"This excellent compilation of the stories of our newest Americans is a study in deprivation, struggle, faith, and the power of the human spirit. I applaud the Minnesota Council of Churches for undertaking this effort in order to share these powerful tales. They serve to instruct us, to educate us. The storytellers overcame great adversity in their lives to become American citizens. May we learn from their courage and strength."

—US Congressman Keith Ellison, representative of Minnesota

"Our stories are sacred; without them, we forget who we are. All respect to the brave beings who survived hells of brutality...and lived to tell us. Bless the messengers in this book; their words can knit our torn and fragmented humanity back together again. Thank you—how can we truly function as a community without knowing one another's stories?"

—Julia Dinsmore, Twin-Cities grandmother, educator, artist, cultural worker, and author

"Here we have stories about our own neighbors who have endured much in coming to this country—leaving their own nation states, land, houses, families, and friends because of the extreme conditions of oppression, persecution, and warfare that they faced. In these stories we find people with the same hopes that we have for ourselves and our families. These stories help us appreciate what refugees have lost and yet what they contribute to our communities when they come here. Beware! These stories will open your heart and your mind toward your neighbor!"

—Sally Dyck, resident bishop of Minnesota, the United Methodist Church

"*This Much I Can Tell You* is a testimony to the suffering and courage of refugees from around the world. Theirs are the stories of persecution, desperation, hope, and human triumph. This collection serves as a reminder that we live in an interconnected world and that geographical and political distances have shrunk. This collection also is a testimony to America and its people, and to its ongoing commitment to open its doors to the world's most oppressed, continuing to weave today's refugees into the rich fabric of our nation."

—Erol Kekic, director of Church World Service Immigration and Refugee Program.

"The moving accounts of uprooted people from around the world embracing opportunities to rebuild their lives in Minnesota shared in this volume remind us why we are so committed to refugee resettlement and to a partnership with our affiliate, MCC Refugee Services. We hope these stories of hardship endured and hope sustained will compel readers everywhere to join us in embracing the gifts of our new neighbors."

—Deborah Stein, director of Episcopal Migration Ministries

"Many of the stories in this profound, haunting, beautiful book seem too hard to read, too hard to bear. But for just this reason they are also potentially transformative and thrillingly redemptive, even magical. Refugees have suffered from war and violence so depraved it can seem surreal. These are the stories of this book and thus one may veer from shock to disgust to disbelief before a surprising turn of the heart occurs. It dawns that a human being has survived all of this butchery and evil and is telling his or her story. What this says about the potential of humanity and about the immensely courageous refugees living now in Minnesota surpasses the power of words to tell. That power, though, is the heart and soul of this book and if one had to choose one word to name that power, one would surely have to call it love."

—Doug McGill, journalist, author, teacher, and founder of the McGill Report

"These stories speak to the bravery, determination, and shared sacrifices of men and women in pursuit of freedom and their dreams. They demonstrate the generosity that exists in families and communities, especially in the worst of situations. *This Much I Can Tell You* vividly captures how these lives start from ordinary and simple beginnings and journey through extraordinary hardships, only to be aided by families and newfound friends and sustained by faith and hope. This book provides an unconditional assurance as these women and men become our next door neighbors, coworkers, and trusted friends in the reshaping of Minnesota and our country."

—Gus Avenido, refugee state coordinator, Minnesota Department of Human Services

"In *This Much I Can Tell You*, unsung heroes share their poignant stories of survival and triumph of the human spirit, offering a deeply humbling experience to Minnesotans who care to witness the depth of courage and strength of character of some of our newest neighbors."

—Linda Glaser, author of *Bridge to America: Based on a True Story* and *Emma's Poem: The Voice of the Statue of Liberty*

"In *This Much I Can Tell You*, refugees detail their experiences, hardships, and dreams as they trek towards their new world. The stories in this book capture important details of refugees from diverse backgrounds in their own voices. Existing narratives of refugees in Minnesota are enhanced by this important work, each story putting a human face to the challenges refugees encounter."

—Yasmeen Maxamuud, author of *Nomad Diaries*

THIS MUCH I can TELL YOU

Stories of Courage and Hope from Refugees in Minnesota

Edited by
Minnesota Council of Churches
Refugee Services

ISBN: 978-0-9848588-0-4
Library of Congress Control Number: 2011928159

Printed in the United States of America
Second Printing: 2011
Cover painting by Aziz, used with permission of WellShare International
Book design by Ryan Scheife, Mayfly Design
15 14 13 12 11   5 4 3 2

Published by Minnesota Council of Churches

Dedication

"Heroes, all of them—the new pilgrims, the refugees. To leave your country for the sake of your children and ship out over the edge of the world to America and venture into the new language that you will not be so comfortable or humorous in as in your mother tongue. My father grew up on a farm in Minnesota, a devout Christian, with powerful family loyalties, and when I look around our country, the people I see who are most like him are the brave strangers who've come to escape cruelty and find dignity and freedom so their kids can have a good life. If we knew their stories, we could not keep back the tears."

—Garrison Keillor © 2011

Table of Contents

Foreword

By Kao Kalia Yang, author of
The Latehomecomer: A Hmong Family Memoir

This much I can tell you…

It is a tough thing to be a refugee in Minnesota, but to be here means that we have a chance at life in very real ways, and so we have journeyed far in the hopes that we may belong. I came when I was just six years old. Shielded by youth and innocence and by the adults around me, I had time to grow up and open my eyes to the world of America in far gentler ways than the many whose stories are in these pages.

I read the words of the men and the women who have survived. I see them on the streets. Women with long hair tied back and men with white shirts carefully buttoned. I hear their voices. Whispers to one another on a crowded city bus, or the sometimes urgent yells of mothers and fathers at the backs of children running in the near distance. There are scars that they carry on their bodies. Inside each: a series of jagged memories, broken emotions, housed within the battered shells. They search, find, lose, and try again for hope and for life—so that the young ones, like I was, like I am, can carry forward the wisdom and the strength of the hardships they have encountered in ensuring that our lives may continue.

What is Somalia? What is Liberia? What is Burma? What is Zimbabwe? What is Ethiopia? What is the Democratic Republic of Congo? What is Iraq? What is Bhutan? What is Cameroon? What is…the place you speak of where you were once positioned for life that was all demolished in a minute of looking, in a moment of being seen, in the push of gravity and the pull of time? All these places become stories. This river was that river. The night of the crossing. The baby on my back. The bullets whizzing by. His cry. My shoulder soaking with wet—sweat? It took a long time for the sticky to register, the heavy ooze, the thickness in between. My baby was sputtering blood. The bullet had gone through his teeth. Lodged there in his tongue, a flash of silver in the opening wound. The sounds of fear shooting forth. These are the stories I have heard. They happen out of the realm of our realities.

What is America? We are sitting on the sofa. We are watching television. They talk and they tell stories of the brothers and sisters we've never met, of the bullets we don't remember, of the hurt that we cannot heal. These places are nightmares in their closed lids, late at night, hearts shivering while we sleep, while we try to dream a path into the future, free our hearts from the weight that pulls so heavily from the past. We are America, we dream of it, each and every night, with or without images, in the dark, our spirits fan out slowly from our bodies and we grow light and we grow wide and we spread ourselves thin all over this country to find our place.

We, the children of refugees, believe that one day—the beautiful day in the future when a warm sun shines and the winds of summer blow and the birds are chirping in their trees and the fish in the water swims, silver streaks hidden in the mirrors of moisture that the pain will not be so fresh anymore, and they can look at us and see how we have survived, how we have sustained, how our stories have changed here in America.

Love is the thread that holds us to their stories. Love is the push and the pull of the words that tangle with the emotions deep inside and purge, bit by bit, the dry salt of tears fallen on the sunken cheeks of despair. In our palms the salts glisten in the light and prisms of courage born, passion reflected as we gaze upon the jewels of wisdom that suffering sometimes brings. In each grain of hurt, there lies the hope of humanity. These stories, this love, is bigger than we are.

And so in these pages, we ask you to share—the gifts of our mothers and fathers and our brothers and sisters from around the world. We ask that you carry in your palms the salt of their tears so that together we can shine light on the broken world that has inspired in us a burn to give birth to wholeness, again. It is the wish for a place where each of us can live, safe in the knowledge that we are where we belong, parts and pieces of a happier story's end.

It is a tough thing to be a refugee in Minnesota, but to be here means that we have a chance at life in very real ways, and so we have journeyed far in the hopes that we may belong.

Acknowledgements

First and foremost, we want to thank the storytellers. Without the willing offerings of their memories we would not have a book. We are immeasurably thankful for those brave enough to revisit the past and share their stories of tragedy and hope with us. They are the heroes of this book and we are honored to be able to document their remarkable histories.

The creation of *This Much I Can Tell You* would not be possible without the generous involvement of the following people: Kristin Ginger, with AmeriCorps VISTA, for initiating this project, conducting interviews, and editing transcripts; and Naomi Thorson Krueger, also with AmeriCorps VISTA, for ushering the book through the publication process, conducting interviews, editing the stories, and writing an introduction and conclusion which put the heart of this work into words.

To Kao Kalia Yang we owe a debt of gratitude. Her own experience is a testimony to the strength of refugees. Her poetic and powerful words in the foreword weave the stories of this book into the narrative of our nation. We are deeply grateful for her contribution.

To Garrison Keillor, an iconic Minnesota storyteller, for providing inspiring words to dedicate this book to the heroes we find in refugees.

We would like to recognize the many volunteers who spent hours transcribing the audio recordings of the interviews. A special thanks to John Ziegler, a faithful MCC Refugee Services volunteer, who researched and wrote the contextual historical introductions for each country.

A heartfelt thank you for the beautiful cover art by the local Somali artist Aziz, used with the permission of WellShare International. This painting is a story unto itself.

And finally, this book was made possible in part by the Arts and Cultural Heritage Fund through the vote of Minnesotans on November 4, 2008. We would like to thank the Minnesota Historical Society for administering this grant and for awarding us the funding for the publication of this book.

—Rachele King
Director of Refugee Services,
Minnesota Council of Churches

Introduction

Since the beginning of time, storytellers have been the keepers of cultures' histories. Whether told around a warm fire in a rural village, sung from a city stage, written on brittle paper, or now captured on media like YouTube, stories have kept memories of previous generations alive in the minds of the next. But what happens when an entire society is, for one reason or another, displaced across the world? The stories of a culture are sometimes all that is left of home when people flee their countries and seek safety in others—often with just the clothes on their backs, the few belongings they could carry, and, if they are lucky, their children and spouses, too.

In our world today there are over fourteen million refugees—people who have fled their countries of origin and are unwilling or unable to return due to well-founded fears of persecution for reasons of race, religion, nationality, membership of a particular social group, or political opinion. And less than half of 1 percent of these people are resettled in a third country—the rest are sent home, integrated into the societies to which they fled, or, in most cases, warehoused in refugee camps for years, decades, or even generations.

Since 1979, Minnesota has welcomed more than ninety-three thousand new refugees and asylees[1] to our state. These people come with hope for a better future and lifetimes of joy and sorrow behind them.

Minnesota Council of Churches (MCC) Refugee Services is an

---

1. Minnesota Department of Health website, "Primary Refugee Arrivals to Minnesota."

1

affiliate of Church World Service and Episcopal Migration Ministries, two national agencies contracted by the US Department of State to resettle refugees domestically. Locally, we partner with volunteers and local faith communities, as well as governmental and nonprofit social services to offer an abundant welcome to Minnesota's newest refugee residents. In this capacity, we interact with people from across the globe, and encounter incredible individuals who are survivors of some of our world's most traumatic circumstances. These remarkable people join local communities that know little about their personal histories, and the refugees themselves often lack the capacity to make their stories known.

This book is our attempt to document some of these stories. Our intent is twofold: to tell the stories of an otherwise silenced population and to give the storytellers an opportunity to own their stories with pride and dignity, and in so doing, experience healing. The people we interviewed were all connected to MCC Refugee Services as clients or staff—former refugees and asylees who have now made their lives in Minnesota. The stories do not represent all refugees of each ethnic group, nor is this collection proportionally representative to the refugee populations in Minnesota. *This Much I Can Tell You: Stories of Courage and Hope from Refugees in Minnesota* is a serendipitous coming together of people willing and able to share the raw memories of their journeys to Minnesota.

When people apply for refugee status before they arrive in the United States—or asylees apply after having already arrived—they must give an account of why they cannot return home. A person tells her or his story multiple times to representatives from the United Nations, the US Department of Homeland Security, and other nongovernmental organizations. This story must resemble closely enough the stories from people in that person's ethnic group and from other family members or she or he risks being blocked from resettlement. This traumatic experience can strip people of the dignity and ownership of their stories, turning them instead into bargaining chips to freedom. As we continued to hear these stories, we grieved what these people had lost.

So we turned on a digital audio recorder and started at the beginning of things—"Tell me about your childhood..." we'd often begin—and let the story flow from the storytellers' earliest memories to the reasons their lives fell apart to how they arrived in Minnesota. We gave each narrator full agency over what she or he chose to tell and what that person chose to keep quiet. Each had final say in what we published and had every right to pull out of the project before the book went to print. We did not question our storytellers' memories of things by cross-checking facts against historical research or other people's stories; this collection is history as each person remembers it. It is a collection of memories—fluid and malleable. As one storyteller begins her story, "Bhutan...it is like a dream." And as another ended his tale, "That much I can tell you." Some of the storytellers chose to use their own names; others have provided pseudonyms. These people are the survivors of persecution and many still have families in their home countries that they must protect, even from a distance.

We hope that *This Much I Can Tell You* will transform not only you, the reader, but also the storytellers themselves, empowering them to raise their voices and add their stories to the collective Minnesota history.

Come, gather around! And listen to these stories of tragedy, courage, and hope for a better future.

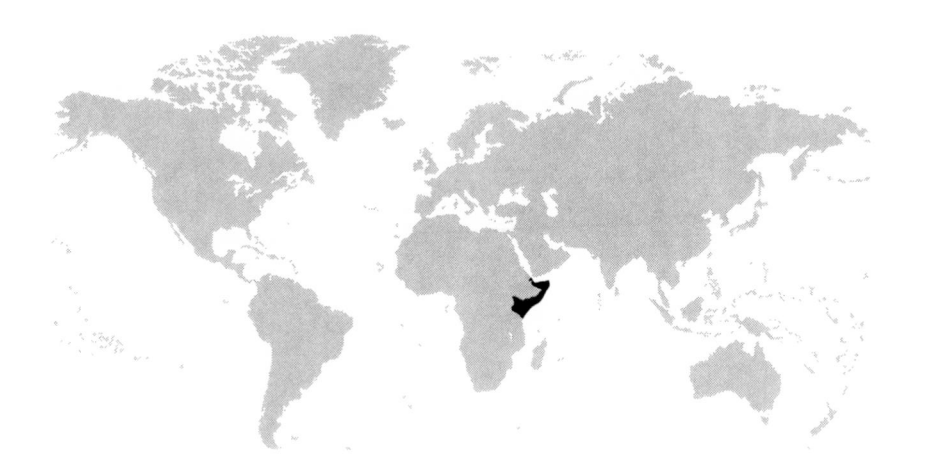

Somalia

Over seventeen thousand Somali refugees have resettled in Minnesota over the past two decades[2], and the Twin Cities are home to the largest Somali population in the United States[3]. Formerly colonized by the British and Italians, a unified Somalia gained its independence in 1960.[4] In 1992, after a severe famine struck the East African nation, the United States military led Operation Provide Relief, airlifting food and other provisions for the Somali people. When the military's mission changed and it attempted to arrest warlord Mohammed Farah Aideed, the humanitarian mission turned violent, and soon the United States withdrew from the country. A series of civil wars followed, and the United States began resettling Somali refugees in 1993.[5]

Somalia, primarily covered by desert and, between monsoons, with hot and humid conditions, still witnesses fighting between various clans and warlords.[6] The country has a population of over ten million, but the

---

2. Minnesota Department of Health website, "Primary Refugee Arrivals to Minnesota."

3. Michelle Knoll, KSTP.com

4. Center for Applied Linguistics website, "Somalis: Their History and Culture,"

5. Al-Jazeera. "From Minneapolis to Mogadishu."

6. CIA World Factbook, "Somalia."

United Nations High Commissioner for Refugees (UNHCR), the United Nations Refugee Agency, reports that there are more than 678,000 refugees of Somali origin living in refugee camps in Kenya, Ethiopia, Djibouti, and Yemen.[7] These refugees primarily speak Somali and practice Islam.[8]

---

7. "Somalia," UNHCR.org.

8. CIA World Factbook, "Somalia."

Sharmake:
Health-Care Worker, Success Story

Twenty-five-year-old Sharmake comes to the MCC office on a day when the air is filled with swirling snow. He is used to sharing his story with people—he is one of the most active members of the Refugee Speaker's Bureau. Sharmake has also volunteered as an interpreter for a few classes at MCC. His story has been featured in the newsletter of MCC Refugee Services' national partner, Episcopal Migration Ministries (EMM); he was interviewed in a documentary by EMM as well. Sharmake has become somewhat of a celebrity at MCC and the relationships he has formed with his case manager and other staff people continues to encourage the entire office. He speaks purposefully, telling his story animatedly.

"I remember I was a kid in Somalia. I was younger. I was living with my family, with my mom and my two brothers, before the civil war. And then I was going to *dugsi*, the Islamic school. *Dugsi* for Qur'an, with my brother. And my mother and my father was having a shop in front of our home. And then also my aunt was living with us."

Sharmake explains that his parents owned a grocery store, which supported their family. Sharmake is the middle of three brothers. As a child, Sharmake remembers the fun he had with his friends.

"I was playing with a ball made by plastic. We played on the beach. I was following the neighbor kids who were my elder. We young people, after we finish *dugsi*, we would play with them. I remember that it was fun to play soccer, plastic soccer. The ball was made by plastic.

"We were living in a city called Kismayo. It was a nice place. When we fled, I was seven years old. One morning, I was hearing some guns, the sound of guns saying that people are fighting together. Earlier in the morning, some bandits came to our home. And then they killed my father. I woke up and my mom was crying over there, outside the apartment. She said what happened and was crying and she held us. We left that place the same evening. When it become dark, like midnight, my mom took us and we come all the way down to the border of Kenya.

"Oh, I was tired. My mom was doing really wise things. When we walked some miles, we would stop and relax. We would take a little bit relax and we would keep walking. We would go from neighbors', to neighbors' homes, and we would feel comfortable. But we weren't going a direct route. We were going through the bush. When we felt tired we would relax and take some tea and some milk, and then we would walk.

"I remember when we come to border, there was army people who had guns. I think it was the government of Kenya. When we come to the border they come to us and tell us to sit down over there. Then they took us to Liboyo, a city on the border. After that, I remember we were living under the tree with my mom and other people who put plastic outside the tree. They made us a house and then we sat in there. And I remember some nights there were some other bandits coming, even at the border, killing people, taking their foods out, raping the women. It was difficult. This was 1992, I remember. I was seven. It was around two months that this was happening. I don't remember; it was almost two months and then we fled to prepared camps in Kenya.

"In the morning, I remember we took a big van and a big truck, my mother and brothers and two of my neighbors traveled with us. A lot of families were there. The truck was full. And then we come all the way down, ninety miles inside to the country of Kenya. There was some Somali refugees who had come earlier in 1991. And there were houses already prepared with roofs and trees. There wasn't any wall; the house was only tree and a roof. And only some plastics on the inside. So actually I think we came at evening time to that place. Then we were told the houses—there were a lot of houses—we were told, 'Everybody catch up!

8

Any room; one family per house.' Then when the truck drove the people and all the people they run to catch an apartment.

"You can pick which one you like. And Mom picked one; it was nice. The one Mom picked was the one we lived, and I was raised there the rest of my life. I was there for eighteen years. It was four meters by three meters and there was a roof. Later on, people were coming until the camp became full. And then you know when we came there, same time, the mom, Hazle and I had the same *dugsi*. I was learning there. For learning Qur'an religion: Islam. And after *dugsi*, there was school established and I go to school.

"I started [learning English with] ABCDE, and I just continued until I just finished my grad. My grad is there. And I was a grown-up in the camps. Later on, you know, when you come to the camps, the bandits were the same. People in United Nations was giving food. Before they were good, they were giving rice; they were giving per person two pounds of flour per person. And they were giving six, like, three people they give six pounds of rice and one liter of oil. It became worse and worse until the rice was gone. And they start giving maize: two pounds of maize per person for fifteen days. That's two weeks. Then life became harsh. They were already distributing only food. Then they told people they didn't have firewood or a machine to cook the food. So the mothers and fathers are going to the bush to take the firewood to cook the food. And you know, when the fathers go out, he would be killed by the bandits. Then they kill. When the women go there, they're going to rape the women. They were raping the women and killing the fathers. At the same time they were coming at nighttime to the camps and they were killing.

"I just remember one night, it was midnight, and I said, 'Mommy, I wanna go outside. I wanna go to bathroom. Mom I want to go to bathroom.' She turned and said, 'Okay.'

"You know there is a toilet outside, a hole in the ground. It was 2:00 a.m. And then the mom saw a light in front of the other apartment. She said, 'Oh, my son, there's something wrong. Let's go back.' I am scared. I am weak for a moment inside. After an hour, my mom was crying. My mom went to the apartment and people come out and she see that one of our neighbors was just shattered in his back. They killed, you know. It was just so close to us. My mom wasn't hearing the gun, she was just seeing the light. Maybe it was when they go out...it came worse by worse by worse.

"That was the life in the refugee camp. They were not having food, or enough shelter even. We were the lucky people. We came when the place had a roof. The people who came after us they were not having any roofs. They are coming, they were only giving the plastic, and they don't have power to build a house. They want to take woods or some trees to build house: bamboos. But if they go outside they will be shot. And they don't have money to buy it. So they are confused. They don't know what to do. They go back to Somalia and they are shot. So I spent my life there. It was eighteen to nineteen years. Nineteen ninety-two to 2010."

All of his memories are not of fear. As a child growing up in a refugee camp, Sharmake was not always aware of the dangers around him. He and his friends had fun, just like they had back in Somalia.

"Sometimes kids don't know something. If they saw one bad thing happen today, tomorrow they don't remember. You know what we did, we just playing. I remember, when we came to the camps, we played the same games. When it was raining outside, we would go play in the rain. And we would take off our shirts and we would run."

Sharmake smiles brilliantly as he reminisces about the fun he and his friends had together. He describes a game they used to play that involved throwing a shoe in the air. If it landed face up, one team would chase the other. If face down, the opposite team would run and be chased.

"That was a fun game we were having. At the school we had fun games, too. Later on I got a soccer ball, and we played that until we grew up. And we learned the people."

But Sharmake didn't always know why he had to live in the camp.

"I was asking some questions to my mom: 'When will we go back to our home?' I was seeing what was happening, but I would say, 'Why is our home here? Can't we leave here? Our house at home was a good, nice apartment.' It was not like bamboos. I would ask my mom—there

10

the place was too hot. I say, 'Mom, we can't live here. Let's go home.' She would say, 'Okay, we'll go back later; not now.' She was building my brain, she was telling me, 'Cool down, son; we will go back one day.'

"That's only what I remember. I just finish my primary school, and I was like, 'Yeah, I know everything that's happening in this refugee camp, this harsh life.'"

Sharmake explains that his mom wove baskets and sold them to make money to support her family. His voice reveals traces of bitterness: he didn't like to see his mother work so hard.

"Nobody is keeping her. She is waiting at the hand of the United Nations. I finished my school and just decide to make a link with NGOs, you know.

"I went there and took classes. I just told them, 'Can I see the coordinator of the place?' That was the time I think, oh man, you can't continue your education because Mom has already become tired. And you've become grown up. You need what to wear, what to eat. And the mom, and the life, became harsh. Nobody is giving you repeal. So I just say, 'Where can you catch up?' I was the only one who was having that opportunity.

"Many of my age-mates were finishing school and they didn't have anything to do. And the United Nations wasn't paying refugee school. They were in market doing things, maybe going back to the war country. You know, you have to build your life, man! So I went to one coordinator of the chairman NGO. I just told him, 'Man, I want to get some experience from your agency so you can help me. You're helping the refugees health program. So just help me get experience in order to be proficient in the future.' He just look at me, 'Young boy. Yeah. You work on that because you were brave.' He just gave me an appointment and told me to come back this day.

"So in two weeks I went back and he told me, 'Oh, you will take a nine month class.'"

Sharmake explains that he was to take the class for nine months, but if after six months he was succeeding, he would be offered a chance to volunteer in the NGO.

Sharmake recounts what the man said to him: "'You will work as a practical. If I see you working and everything, I will hire you.' They gave me classes. The first three, four months, he just came back to me. 'Young boy, I want you to go with this guy and follow him every morning. You have to record everything he say.' There was no machine to copy, you know. When he prescribed the drugs, I just take paper and record whatever he writes. The patient takes a prescription or the doctor, and he comes and I see it, he brings the description, and I write his name, his block, where he live, his drugs he is taking, his diagnosis, probably.

"The first four months I start working like that. Second, after I was volunteering for six months, he said, 'Young boy, follow this guy. With immunization program, you know, he is giving vaccination. You have to learn how to manage the vaccines and everything. Packing vaccines. Just follow him, working as a volunteer only. And just packing vaccines. You know, ice packs.' He told me, 'We need an experienced person in this place, instead of hiring ignorant person. You need to learn the vaccines and we will hire you.'"

Sharmake explains that he volunteered for GTZ Health, a German organization. After he was a student for nine months, he was "hired" as a volunteer.

"I was assistant. Refugee people they call assistant. They only employ people from Kenya who are educated. I was low; I was in low grade, you know. Assisting them with everything. Until the end, I just adapted. I was working. You know, you can see, my last thing I was doing, I was managing all vaccines in the camp. Mornings I follow a vehicle, then I drop the vaccines, then I go to main hospital. I was collecting the vaccines, I was dropping at each health facility. We were calling hospitals. Each camp, each section, has one health care. It's called *health post*. Actually, the camp was having five, like five health posts and one main hospital. So I become—after that I become full, doing everything. Getting a lot of experience.

"I was working five years. Until I came to the United States. I just resigned when I came here. I was working every opportunity, classes, every scholarship opportunity. I was the first person there. I just take some trainings, like HIV/AIDS, and how to prevent—how to prevent the mother to child with the HIV. It's called PMCT. At the same time, I became counselor. When the doctors know they have it, I was counseling mothers about HIV/AIDS, prevention for the kid. That she can save the kid 80 percent if she delivers at hospital. You know, many people traditionally don't deliver at hospital. Rather than delivering at hospital they like to deliver at home. All Somalis. I know Somalis here who go to the doctor. But in their home country, in the refugee camp, all mothers like to deliver at home instead of the hospital.

"In 2008, I got another part-time job. I was cashiering customers. I was doing good. The last years in refugee camp was really doing good, you know. Though some people were doing worst, but I was the only, I can say I was the only one who was earning something. You know how many I was earning? I was earning for the month? Fifty dollars. Sixty dollars. And it seems this is the highest grade. When I had the two jobs, money was one hundred something dollar. Kenya money is like seven, eight thousand Kenyan money, shilling money. But when you imagine it to the America dollar, it is like one hundred dollars. Yeah." Sharmake says that he was the primary financial provider for his family with the money he earned.

Now Sharmake explains the confines of living in a refugee camp.

"You know the camp is square, you know. It's like around three hundred. I don't know the circle. The circle place where the United Nations pulled from the government of Kenya. They deal together; you know they pay money. That place, nobody can go out from that camp. All people are there. If you go out from one mile from the camp, you will be asked to bring ID. ID in Kenya is called *kitanbulosho*. They cannot travel anywhere. They cannot go back to country because there is a war. The government of Kenya is serious, because only here is the refugee camp. They cannot go out from the camp. They are in ache, you know. They are in a prison; the outside is open. You can't move.

"There was no fence, but you can't go outside the border. If you go to Somalia, people are killing people. If you go to Kenya, the government

13

of Kenya will arrest you. They will ask for your ID. And then, you know, people are stressed. People are talking to themselves. You can see a person walking on the road talking to himself, saying, 'I need this, this...' You wonder, you look back, you can say, 'What is this guy doing?' You can say he is talking to himself. Nobody with him. People are depressed. Stressed. Talking to themselves. They go to this side they will be killed," Sharmake says, motioning to the right. "They go to this side they will be killed," he says and motions to the left.

"They don't have enough food. They don't have enough water. They don't have enough health care even. There was only the one agency, and there were more than three thousand, more than two hundred thousand refugee people and only one health agency. Kids are malnourished. Kids, you know, need milk, vegetables to grow up. They are not getting that. They are only getting maize and oil. They become malnourished. I really can't imagine the life there. They are not living in good houses. Raining time is coming and people are feeling chilly. Though the place is very hot, it is like a desert.

"The equator is in the middle. Kenya is the middle place where the world equator passes. When the world is circle like this,"—Sharmake draws a circle with his finger on the table—"Kenya is in the middle. It is a very sunny place. Kenya is very hot. People are in plastic you know. When the sun hits the plastic, you know, people feel hot. They can't sleep daytime. And the plastic scorch, you know. When the rain come, the rain comes inside, you know. They don't have enough, you know, education; they don't have work. It's rare to get a job; it's rare to get the high education.

"That was really life: not enough water, people fighting. You can see people losing their life only to get water. They go in a line early in the morning getting water, you know. Just kill each other, they say, 'I was first! No, I was first!' And then they kill each other, you know; they lose their life, you know."

Sharmake now explains the process of applying for resettlement, and his frustration with the interview process required for approval to be sent to a new country. He says that the UN gave people a lot of hope, offering them the possibility of leaving their harsh lives and moving on to something new.

"You know what happened? They interviewed fifty families. He just interviewed the people and he say, 'Where you come from?' and 'What's your name?' You know, but he can't tell his full name, you know, because he's depressed, he's afraid, his family was killed in front of him, his parents was maybe killed in front of him his houses his money was all taken out, you know. And then he don't know what war he's talking about and he's the head of the family."

Sharmake explains that it can be very difficult to recount the past, especially if traumatic events have muddled one's memories. He says many people have to go through a second interview, and they fail if they do not answer the questions the same way they did the first time.

"He's depressed; he don't know what he's talking about, you know. And then he fails. You know when he failed, he get another stress, or his family, the rest of the family, they stress, you know. They were having hope to go to United States or to go to European country like England or like that. And then they were rejected. Then all the family will be shocked, maybe the family, one person was depressed before after they were rejected, maybe it's 70 percent of the family become—will become—stressed and depressed, you know. That has a problem now that they are in for the last few years."

"The process take one year for us. First we find the UN and my mom say something; I was with her, I was copying. Whatever she says, I was writing down. I did a great job, whatever she says. Then the clerk told me, 'Hey guy, what are you doing?' I just say, 'I'm writing down what my mom says because I know she have seen something bad in home country, maybe she cannot remember the next interview. You want to interview her the next day, but maybe she'll not remember. I'll write down and next day when we are coming here, maybe I'll tell her whatever she say that day. I'll try to remember.' He told me, 'Don't write down, but have in your mind.'

"I cannot oppose, because if I oppose I may lose my opportunity. So I just close the paper and I was listening in my head what the mom say. After he finish the interview, I just tell my elder brother to copy whatever my mom says, and after two minutes, we write down whatever he say and how she answered.

"For the next interview, I just told the mom everything. I recite to her—I recited everything. I tell my mom, 'You tell them this, you tell them this, just remember this, this, this.' And that day he told us to listen to what Mom say and the next day he want to interview us, ourselves. And we don't know where something that happen in home country, you know. I say okay, we talked, we write down, we tell my brother, I tell my mom everything. Second interview, we pass the same; he ask me the same question and my mom replied the same, and us replied the same. I, and after that we send—we were send our case to United Nation[s] embassy and—yeah, yeah American Embassy—then we are approved. That was a happy day that we are approved to United States, then we are safe; the government of United States took your case and they interviewed you."

Sharmake says that after three months, his family submitted their case to one final agency: "Criminal investigation or homeland securities to interview you the last. If you pass this interview, it will be fine for you."

In December 2009, they were called in for the Department of Homeland Security interview.

"He was a nice guy. I can't forget that guy who interviewed us. He just called down—he just called once and he told us we'll interview separate: separate Mom, separate with me, separate with my brother separate. Then we just say the same thing, he called the mom. I just say [to] Mom, 'You told me everything and your kids and your family is all same. I wish you change your life to better life,' you know?"

After his mom was interviewed, Sharmake went in for his own interview. "I just told him this process I have been waiting a long time, you know? Long years, you know? And I spend my life in a refugee camp and this is my case. I tell him, 'I think you are the only one who can decide my case to make me pass and you know everything I told you was about my life.' So I said, 'Can you do me a favor? Give me approval.' He just laughed, he just told me, 'Okay, you'll be alright.'"

Then Sharmake went through a medical screening before he could be cleared to come to the United States.

"They check all the blood, everything. Before I was given approval letter from CIS [US Citizen and Immigration Services], I do the medical. That shows that I was already approved, you know? At the same time, while I'm in the medical place, somebody called the name of our family and he gave to us the envelope saying that the government of the United States approved your case for your family and you got accepted to United States. I say, 'Perfect! It's good!' And we pass medical, everything, and then we fixed a flight." Sharmake grins as he tells this part of his story, happiness ringing in his voice. "And my mom came here first. She came here in February 2010, February 25, I came here March 12, 2010 and my brother came in May. He come here and, *Alhamdulillah*,[9] we are living together now. We are okay now. Yeah. That was my process to United States."

Before leaving for the United States, Sharmake and the other refugees who were to be resettled attended a predeparture orientation with people from the United Nations. He went to Nairobi, Kenya, for this orientation, and during it he watched a video about what to expect in the United States. Sharmake says that he learned, among other things, about the police and the tasks he would need to accomplish during his first week in the United States.

"I just finish my week orientation. My worst thing in orientation was the guy who gave the lesson about working in United States. The trouble of United States and how to spend the money you know? He turned on music and then he just put—he just put three seats in the middle and he turned the music on and he told five of our member to dance, to go around the chairs. We go around, 'round, 'round; then he turn off the music. We were five people to sit in three seats. The first person will sit that seat, you know. We just go 'round, 'round, 'round; he turned off. Three, four, five. I

---

9. An Arabic phrase meaning, "All praise is due to Allah."

was fighting to get a seat, you know. He turned off and I just take my seat, you know; the other two, they are losers. He said 'Okay, you three go on.' He took away one seat; two seats left. Then he said, 'Go around, three of you.' We go 'round, 'round, then he turn off the music. Then I become the loser: two other people get the two seats, you know. Then the left two, he turned on the music again and he just took out one seat and he left one seat. He just say, 'You go around, you people; you two go around, then one person want to sit the seat.'

"He said, 'Do you know why I'm doing this?' We said no. He said, 'The trouble of United States is like this: you have to find…it's like, lucky by lucky. One person get the job; other person cannot get the job.'"

Sharmake was disappointed to learn that finding a job in the United States would be so difficult.

"The next lesson was about spending money. He said, 'Okay, you get a job. You start at eight dollars.' He calculated; he said one month is one thousand dollar. Then he minus electricity bill, minus rent, minus your food, minus everything, leave zero money. I just say, 'What the heck!? I'm working four weeks, forty hours and getting one thousand dollar and then I'm spend all of things in—what you think, man?' And he said, 'When you go there, you'll see. People are working only to pay the bills, nothing else,' he said. 'Unless you have a great high education.'"

That day, they left Kenya and flew to New York, where Sharmake and the other refugees resettling in the United States stayed together in a hotel. The next day, they were separated and sent across the country to various states.

"I was the only one going to Minnesota. Nobody else was with me. I was thinking my mom is there. She will be in front of the airport, you know?

"And I come all the way down to the airport, the airport of Minneapolis, Minnesota, but I was confusing looking outside. I just see a guy come to me. I just came up the exit with my bag. I see the mom and my sister, they run to me,"—Sharmake claps his hands together—'Oh, Mom, you're here!'

"Someone from the Minnesota Council of Churches took the mom and my sister to airport, you know, and then we followed together from the plane. Then I was brought to my apartment. I was told, 'This is your apartment; just take it. Here is your bathroom,' where I wasted a lot of gallons. My mom told me, 'This is the bathroom where you can take bath, use the tub.' I just I wasted—oh, my—I wasted a lot of water. This is a lot of water. It takes only one gallon to take a bath in the camp, you know? So I take shower; I just remember where the water—I say, man, how many gallons are you wasting now? And people in the refugee camp"—Sharmake's voice drops to a whisper—"they are not even able to get water. I just say, it's life changing. I just came out and I adapted."

Sharmake says that he was connected with a volunteer named Linda who helped him get acclimated to his surroundings.

"She took me to school where I start my English-building classes, ESL, and I just continue. I just finish my ESL class. Now, I am now in transition class. Yeah, I can go now to college or I can go anywhere. Anything I want to do now, I can! Anything I like. A lot of people help, but as you know, Minnesota Council of Churches is the one that helped us." Sharmake lists several names of people who work at MCC Refugee Services. "You know, a lot of people helped us. A lot of agency came to us, you know, and help us like that. I just finish my eighth month now and then they told me after eight months, you have to find a job.

"I got a job was sorting parts. I was sorting the parts then, I record in my sheet, then I put the data in the computer. It took one month and fifteen days, then the work stopped you know. I was finished. That was a temporary job. I just say okay, I just saved some money. I just saved some money and paid my rents, you know. And pay the pass. One of friends of mine going out of the state; he's going to—he's going to Alaska. He told me, he just told me 'Give me some money and I give you my car' because he wants to fish.

"Then now, he give me his car and with his car now I am driving. I'm going to school morning and afternoon. English classes, and mathematic, you know, and when I get this next year I wanna study my nursing classes. I was approved to start my nursing classes. To be nursing assistant. CNA, like certified nursing. I wanna study certified nursing assistant. I wanna start general with that up to—up to March, and I finish that one semester I can work at the hospital and residents; after that I can take my two years RN nurses and I can be a full nurse. After that, I can take four years for doctor. That's my dream, you know.

"Because I was working as a medical, you know, work for my beginning of my life I start medical, you know. I wanna be a doctor. That is what I was dreaming."

Sharmake says that although he can't go back to Somalia to resettle, he wants to help refugees by caring for their health.

"I know the life of refugees, you know. That's why I wanna learn and work with refugees, helping refugees. I want to be part of that, because I want to do a great job with the refugees. I know their life, you know. I was grown up there. I just spend the rest of my life in refugee camp and I wanna assist them."

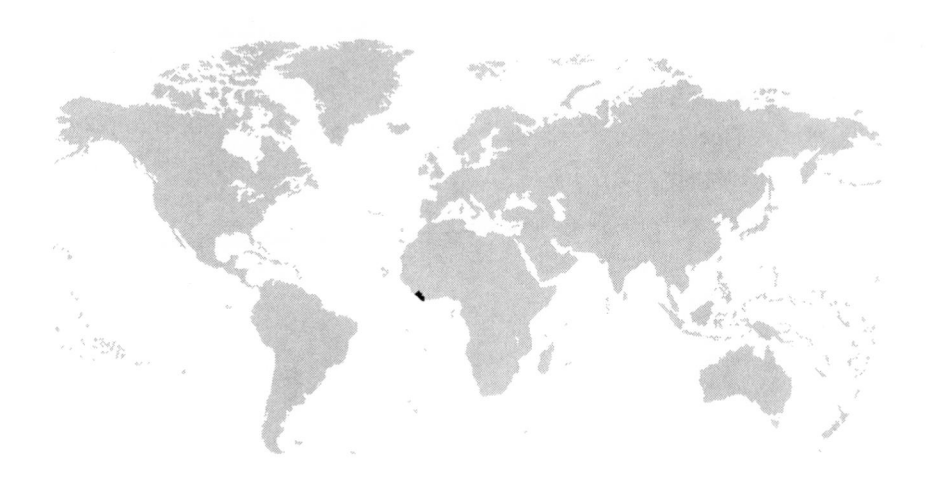

Liberia

Liberia is a West African nation whose population is comprised of a mix of indigenous Liberians and descendants of former American slaves who returned to Africa in the mid-1800s.[10] More than seventy thousand refugees have fled Liberia,[11] and nearly four thousand have settled in Minnesota since 1991.[12]

Many refugees began fleeing after Samuel Doe came to power as the result of a military coup on April 12, 1980. His administration cracked down on the press and political opposition, committed human rights abuses, and allegedly rigged an election in 1985 to retain power. Liberians received no relief when Charles Taylor, who led an invasion of Liberia from the Ivory Coast in 1989, assumed the presidency in 1997. The country remained engulfed in civil war, with atrocities committed daily.[13]

Many Liberian refugees lived in refugee camps throughout West Africa.[14] As did ancestors who were either indigenous people or African-Amer-

---

10. Center for Applied Linguistics, "Liberians: An Introduction to their History and Culture."

11. UNHCR.org, "Liberia."

12. MN Department of Health, "Primary Refugee Arrivals to Minnesota."

13. Center for Applied Linguistics, "Liberians: An Introduction to their History and Culture."

14. UNHCR.org, "Liberia."

ican slaves, some Liberians today speak English and practice Christianity, while others speak indigenous languages and practice Islam or traditional African religions.[15]

---

15. CIA World Factbook, "Liberia."

Moses:
Strong Man, Victim of Torture

Moses tells his story at his house on the last day of September. He lives with his family in the upper half of a duplex. He was born in Maryland County, Liberia, and begins his story by saying that his parents were rice farmers.

"I went to the capital for high school," he elaborates, "but every vacation I went home to my parents." His parents had nine children; one of his two sisters has died, and two of his six brothers were killed during wartime.

After high school, his father passed away, and Moses says, "I couldn't get any support to continue. I started to find a job that I would be doing to support myself. Actually, meantime, I got in contact with a beautiful girl. And we started making family."

"Her parents took her to live with an aunt," Moses says. "The aunt took her to the village to see the rest of the family members, and that's the time that I saw her. I became friends with the little strange girl. It's like I was in contact with a foreigner. We had a certain rock where we used to play, big rock, climb and roll, just roll down. I was sixteen."

Moses continues, "After that, we separated. Her parent took her. Myself, I went with one of my uncles, living with one of my uncles in a little area. And in 1972, we met in the capital. She was going to school. My uncle carry me in to register [for school], and there I met her. She said she saw me and she came out of class and greeted each other. But then we again separated. I didn't know where she went to.

"At the end of that same year, '72, I saw her [and we] started to live

23

together. She couldn't get any good support. Myself, [I] couldn't get any good support. But we decided to live together, because of our love for each other. At that time, I was not living as a saved man." Moses is now a devout Christian.

Finally, Moses found a job doing construction for the government. He says "[My wife] was working for the same government, working in ministry of education for radio operating. She was a radio operator." Moses traveled from county to county in order to work at various government construction sites. He says, "[I went] anywhere they got project."

"Now: civil war." Moses's voice is calm and measured. "At that time, I was in Zwedru, the capital city of Grand Gedeh County. My aunt was in Zwedru; I live in her house. I come from her house and go to work. There, the government carried me to do some construction. It was hard, but it was fine.

"But once you work for the government, during that time, you became a target. Once they have formed your identity...any people getting to government activities will be killed. I was not political!" His tone is absolute. "I was just a government employee."

"Then,"—and now his voice is tense—"the rebels came, going from county to county, capturing counties. Who are these rebels? Rebels who are friends. Friends that we work with. People that we live with. But they decided to turn from us...and go to kill us. And so they started to kill people. We knew that they were coming, but we were told that Zwedru was under protection, that they were not gonna enter. The government said...if you leave, it means that you are a rebel.

"There were government soldiers, very large soldiers [in Zwedru when the rebels came]. There was a lot of fighting, lot of fighting. The soldiers came out and said 'We drove them away! Woo hoo!' they say, jubilating. Two days and *a ba-ba-ba-bap*"—Moses mimics the sound of gunshots and claps his hands—"the rebels came around. They were shooting on the other end while another group [was shooting in a different place], so they could come from four, five different areas and enter.

"The government [soldiers]—they fled. Some of them took their clothes and some took [or] hid their guns. We are confused. We are civilians. In the house, some hid ourselves, some run, or hiding. Once you decide to leave, [the rebels] accuse you of being part of the government, and they will kill you.

"Everyone ran in different directions. Everybody fled the house. Myself, fly. So I never knew where [my aunt and other family from Zwedru] were; they never knew where I was.

"One of my brothers was living in Zwedru, going to school. They caught him and they killed him. His name was Daniel. Daniel was killed. He had a girlfriend, and he decided to keep the Krahn[16] girl's brother. When the rebels came, they are looking for the government employees and they are looking for the Krahn, the Krahn tribe, 'cause the president came from the Krahn tribe. So the Krahn decided to beat together any other tribe—there are thirteen tribes—any other tribe, they look at you suspicious.

"My brother was caught. And they asked him to tell them, 'Where is your brother, Moses?' He say, 'I don't know.' They say, 'Tell us!' He say, 'I don't know.'

"The commander, he say, "Nobody gonna use bullet on this dog.' So they tie him up. They call it *tabey*.[17] They join your elbow with your back. Then they start to slaughter him. They cut your head off and set your head on your chest.

"I don't know how they got to know where I was hiding. They found me." The rebels asked Moses if Daniel was his brother. He replied, "Who Daniel?"

They took him to the house. "I see my brother laying there with his head sitting on his chest."

There is a long silence. "Why?" Moses asks. "He's a student. Why? They were looking for the government. He's a student!" After Moses saw his brother's body, he heard the rebels say, "Knock him down." When

---

16. The Krahn ethnic group, living in Liberia prior to the formation of the country in 1847 by the Americo-Liberians.

17. *Tabey* is a form of torture used during the Liberian civil war that involves tying the person's arms behind his or her back, at the elbows. See the Amnesty International 1995 Report on Liberia article citation.

Moses came to, he described what he heard. "[I] woke up tied. 'Ay! Ay! Ay!' They [the rebels] are killing. 'Ay! Ay! Ay!'" He mimics the screams and shouts.

"They cut your feet, your arms...when they cut your foot here, like that—" Moses gestures toward his ankles—"they are long trousers. Here, short pants." He gestures to just above his knees. "Here, short-sleeve shirt." He gestures to his upper arm. "If they cut here, they are long sleeves." He gestures to his wrist.

Then Moses's turn came. "They say, 'Okay, give him long pants; let him wear long pants.' And so this fellow, he chose to do it. They don't do it at once...He will cut, then he will go and dance. They got blood in a bucket and they dip and drink it. They will come back and start with the other foot.

"While they are doing it, the government came...they started fighting each other." Moses escaped. Despite the open wounds on his legs, the scars of which are still very visible, he managed to make the weeklong journey—on foot—to Maryland County, where his family lived.

Moses survived the trip by taking on a survivor's mentality. "You just drink water. You see any tree, fruit that looks pretty, you just try it and eat it, you know. You just taste it, you just eat. You can be in a group, and if you are not satisfied with the group, then you deviate. You leave them and go your own way. They have to go different directions.

"I went to my house. It was empty. It was empty. Those who decided not to run—there are some people who decided not to go. When you leave your house, they ransack it, take your belongings, total your house. There was nothing left."

There, in Maryland County, someone told Moses that his family had gone toward the Ivory Coast. "Those that fled from Grand Gedeh told my family that I was killed. When they kill the wife, or they kill the husband, they will find the children, they will find the wife, and kill them. Make sure they go down the whole generation. Why? Because they are afraid of revenge. If I know that the rebel kill my dad, I will pick up gun and go fight. So they just go down the line. That's how they work."

Afraid of this and believing Moses was dead, his family had fled.

Moses decided to follow them, but he encountered difficulty in the Ivory Coast. "They speak French. I could not speak French. But there is the Grebo ethnic group [in both] Liberia and the Ivory Coast. So I could understand the native language. I met somebody who spoke Grebo—distant away I could hear it, hear him speaking. I spoke Grebo because my wife's uncle lived in the Ivory Coast."

The man who spoke Grebo didn't know where Moses's family was— thousands of Liberians were fleeing to the Ivory Coast—but was able to tell him where there were others who spoke Grebo.

Moses finally found his wife and seven of their children and he described where they were living. "A little room that everybody was squished in. One room." When he joined them, all eight stayed in that room. "Sometime when we sleep, lay down, there was no room for anybody to enter, no room for anybody to come out.

"We stayed with [my wife's uncle] for a year. We used to get the ration, the food, and some financial aid." After a while, they were able to find a slightly larger room, but there was no way to work to improve their circumstances. "Thirteen years I live in the refugee camp, I never work. Refugees are not allowed to. [Except for] only a small few who were doing contract with UNHCR.

"I became a farmer. There was a UN appeal to the citizens, and they give a swamp. We learn to plant swamp rice. From 1992 to 2003. Yes, I was doing farming. I became a pastor in the refugee camp. Pentecostal."

In 1997, before becoming a pastor, Moses became a deacon. Then he trained with a pastor, but the pastor did not stay. "[He] decided to go back to Liberia because things were a lot easier there with him. But for me, I was still afraid, because the rebels became government. You understand? The rebel leader Charles Taylor, he was no longer rebel leader but he declare himself president. The rebels became government soldiers.

"Charles Taylor is not the only one there, but the lady, Ellen Johnson-Sirleaf, she's the president now. She *is* a rebel. I'm sorry to say that. But she financially assisted Taylor. She and Taylor are the same. But because of US supporting her, that is why she is there, so I don't want to go live with her, so I'm not going there."

In December of 2003, civil war broke out in the Ivory Coast. "The Ivory Coast government accused Liberia of supporting the rebels. The rebels accused Liberia of helping the government. The government said, 'No, we don't need people here [in refugee camps], because you are helping the rebels.' The rebels say, 'You are helping the government.' So we are come and trapped.

"It was impossible. We could not go back to Liberia, but the government in Ivory Coast doesn't want us there. So we went to UNHCR compound. Some fled back to Liberia, some went and came back. When the tension [is] heavy on you, you will cross to Liberia. When the tension in Liberia is not conducive, you will come back to the Ivory Coast. Some decide to be still. Ivory Coast continued to say, 'You guys, we don't want you here; you need to leave.'

"We used to fast, fast, and pray. On one Wednesday morning, my wife and the church members went to the church as usual. But this time [the Ivory Coast soldiers] decided to say, 'No, this is wartime; it's not time to pray.'

"Who will stop this war? How will the war stop?" Moses demands. "We are praying for God to bring peace, because this is the place we are; we consider this to be our home, for the past thirteen years. So we are not praying for rebel. We do not know the rebel, but we pray.

"I was not there—I was at UN office—when they caught the group with my wife. Because my church was one of the biggest churches, they found I could organize. So I became the deputy to the refugee chairman.

"I was sent for and I came, got the UN involved. It took a complete day, whole day, to talk, talk, talk. Finally they say, 'Okay, well, the only thing we can do—this lady, she is the head of this group, we don't want her here today.'

"Since it six o'clock, we cannot cross the border. We say, 'Give us time till tomorrow morning.' They say, 'Yes, we give you time until the morning.' Six o'clock they took my wife and three of the children. But some [of the children] decide be with me. I carry some. She was deported back to Liberia by force. And I was left in Ivory Coast.

"I could not go back to Liberia. I was afraid. Constantly people were yelling that I preach or talk against the rebels. But I was speaking from the Bible. You have no right to take anybody's life away. And that's a fact! That's biblical! God is the maker. He is the creator. He got plan for each and every one of us.

"[My wife] was in danger. She could not stay in Maryland County, so the UNHCR carry her to Monrovia, the capital city of Liberia."

It was after this that Moses began the process of coming to the United States.

"In the camp, I never knew that I would come to the US. But I was there hoping that something would come one day my way. I kept trusting the Lord. I kept depending on him."

The US government had decided to accept a limited number of Liberian refugees. To start this process, Moses had to go through screening in the Ivory Coast's capital city, Abidjan. "We stayed there three months. First they will take your story and they will make record, and pass the record to immigration. So immigration will have the record with you, then they will cross-examine you. From what you told the people from the story, if there is anything different from when you explain it—" Moses throws his hands up in the air.

"Lot of people were not qualified. I was, from what I said, selected. While we were being processed there, the entire war break out in Monrovia. So my wife ran from Monrovia and brought two of the children she carried. Then she was looking for the others. One is in Europe. One son went to Guinea; my oldest one, we never knew where he was. He was in the forest; she got him from the forest, where they were digging gold, digging gold.

"So I brought three [of our children to the US]. Then she found [the other children]. When she got them, I went to MCC. Rachele,[18] she file my petition for them."

Moses's oldest child, a daughter, had already come to the United States in 2002.

"She was found dead in her apartment before I came. She was my

---

18. Rachele King, director of refugee services at Minnesota Council of Churches.

firstborn. They said [it was a] natural death." Moses's sentences become short. "She was found after one week. In 2004, March 2. She was found dead in her apartment. After one week. So they kept the body until I arrive here. But I couldn't see it. Because they were decompose, you know, so I just saw the casket. She died March and I got here May. So they kept the body until I arrive here. I arrive, one week after I arrive she was buried. Buried.

"It was difficult for me. That time, I was discouraged, to be frank, I was discouraged that happen. I could not manage it. And same time [I was living in] the Mayflower house where you live for three months.[19]

"I was looking for a job. I got an overnight job at Sam's Club with my job counselor. We stock the stock." Moses is still at Sam's Club, and, at the time of this telling, is also working at Open Arms of Minnesota.[20] "It is difficult. Difficult to work in the night, and work in the day. It's rough." Moses's wife joined him with another two children. "One of my sons, whether he is living or dead, I don't know." Another three are still in Liberia, but are too old to qualify for the family reunification program.

"I miss preaching. I recently joined a church, and they are trying to work things out so I could preach again. If I could, I want to go to school, to seminary. But I am paying loans, the money that brought us, so this is the thing I am working on. I paid four of all five of us that came first."

Almost all of Moses's children are going to school. He has one in preschool, one in middle school, two in high school, and one at Minnesota Community and Technical College. Moses says, "We are learning the culture here together. They speak our Liberian language and they are now learning the American accent."

"We decided to be here for the rest of our life. Even though I still have passion, I still want to go home because there are a lot of people who still need to know the Lord. All they know now is fighting. Fighting has

---

19. The Mayflower House was a house owned by the Mayflower Community Church and used by Minnesota Council of Churches as temporary low-rent housing in emergency situations until 2009.

20. Open Arms of Minnesota is a nonprofit organization that prepares and delivers nutritious meals to individuals with serious and life-threatening diseases.

become the order of the day. My mom is still there, my sister, my brothers. My mother is there. I support her from here.

"My dream is to go to college, and I want to be a pastor fulltime. My wife is also a minister, so eventually we want to open a church. All this takes money. Seminary takes money, college takes money...I am daily looking for any direction, any scholarship daily." Two of his children will soon be looking at colleges. "We'll see who come out, will help. But you know, we keep our trust in the Lord.

"I don't like...I'm a strong man." In fact, Moses's last name means "strong man." "And I don't like to beg, 'Please give, please give.' The only person I can beg is God, to give me strength and give me good health, that I will be healthy and work. I [am] sure that he will speak to somebody to help us. But I will not look up to man for man to help me. If God speak to man to help me, I appreciate it."

Semantics:
Bold Critic, Committed Journalist

Semantics King Jr. is an asylee from Liberia whose story has been told many times to groups of people at churches, schools, and other events for the Refugee Speakers Bureau. In each retelling of his life story, Semantics explains the reason his father gave him his name. Once again he tells the legend behind his name and the legacy it has brought him.

"[My father] explained that he had some American friends he worked with at the Firestone rubber plantation company in Harbel, [Liberia]. They were from the US, and as they all worked together in the factory, he would always use terminologies; he wouldn't use simple words. Trying to show off, you know. Until his friends said you should have been called Semantics. His friends kept calling him Semantics instead of Jeremiah. And so officially he was Jeremiah King, you know, but his friend kept calling him Semantics. He said, 'Well, I'm going to transfer this name to my son; he's going to grow up with it.' So I was named after him.

"The majority of the people [in Harbel] work for Firestone. My father was in a sort of higher-up position, but as he told me, he felt he did work for his boss and his boss took the credit. Eventually, they had friction between the two of them, and he threatened his boss. So then there was fear in him that since he threatened his boss he would be fired, so eventually he left the company and ran to the military base for the armed forces of Liberia. He joined the army in 1980, [when] I was about two years old."

Semantics explains that his father rarely came home after he joined the army because he was based in Monrovia; his mother would occasionally go to visit him.

"My mother was a stay-at-home mom. She took care of me, then eventually my sister who came next to me, another sister, and a brother. I'm the oldest. I spoke to them today, this morning. They're fine, but they want money in all the troubles.

"As things went on, [my father] went to Monrovia and bought land and built a house for us. That was in '91 because the revolution, as they called it then, erupted in 1989. Younger people were conscripted by the various rebel groupings. The armed forces of Liberia were divided. There were certain elements that held loyalty to their tribes, not necessarily to the president. The armed forces has as its primary responsibility the protection of the sovereignty of the nation, whether that means protecting the president, the people, the land—it is inclusive of everything. But there were those who said the army did not protect the people, and the army used to go and fight the rebels.

"My dad eventually was like, 'Well, I think they're using mostly younger recruits right now, so I don't think they need us yet.' Even the armed forces of Liberia wanted to begin recruiting young boys to go and fight. So my dad said, 'Let me go and stay home, then, and visit the kids.' And he decided to go back to the house he built. Once in a while he came to the military barracks if they needed his services.

"In '91, after the war subsided temporarily, the current senator of Nimba County, Prince Johnson, broke away from Charles Taylor. He captured many suburbs of Monrovia, which included where my dad built our house.

"According to my neighbors, including members of the Liberian Lutheran Church, he went out asking for people that worked in the government. They told me that Prince Johnson and his group went to look for my father. They found him, and they told him to come. The bishop even came out, and they said, 'We're not going to do anything to him; we just want him to escort us.'

"As they walked, [the neighbors] heard a gun sound. And that was the end, you know. When they found the body—according to what I was told—some of the neighbors helped to bury him, because then there were bodies all over and no one cared. At that time, in 1991, I was not very big—about thirteen years old. I had a birthday approaching.

"My mom was in Harbel, so I was in Monrovia with my aunt, who didn't have any children. My mom and aunt arranged that I would be with [my aunt], helping her. Until this day...I had come from school, and my aunt is like, 'Well, let's go. We need to see him [your father] for issues regarding your school.'

"The neighbors told us not to enter the house, told us that it was improper—they tried to hide it from me, in fact; they didn't want to tell me. They called my aunt over. I insisted [to know]. I was like, 'What's happening?' Because I couldn't find my dad.

"And so the Lutheran members told us the story, because my dad used to go to the Lutheran church. They advised us that it wouldn't be safe for us to venture around that area, so we went back. And...that was the end of him."

Semantics says it was a possibility that Prince Johnson and his group would come for their family. "What would a thirteen-year-old boy do to anybody? But yeah, that was a possibility, as I later on discovered."

Immediately after the death of his father, Semantics suffered another trauma. "There was a war waged on the residents of Monrovia by Charles Taylor. He had captured 95 percent of the country. Rumor had it that America wanted to recognize him, but they wouldn't until he could capture the capital city, Monrovia. On October 15, 1992, I was in class. He waged a war. We all scattered from school. We whose parents didn't have cars, we got in the bus. When it subsided, I went home, only to find that my aunt was not there. I didn't know where she went; I was left alone. I just stayed in the house, wondering what had happened, you know—wondering about the possibility of me seeing my aunt and eventually my mom.

"There was a complete breakdown of transportation between Monrovia and Harbel. There were curfews, and the road was blocked. No way to go to Harbel, no way to come to Monrovia. So that separated me from my mom...but I didn't consider that a separation, because I felt that within that process [of violence], my mom and siblings were dead.

"There wasn't any way that I could find them. I did go to find them, and asked neighbors, who said, 'Oh, we don't know where they are. Why would we know where they are?' So I returned to Monrovia. I reckoned that I was an orphan, and if I was to succeed, I had to shoulder the responsibilities on my own.

"I was left to decide for myself, to live and grow up the way I thought would be best for me. I regret many days, you know. I was telling someone this afternoon that if there is anything I regret in my career, I regret that I wasn't born in America, or brought to America when I was five, or, say, ten. I was a young man growing up without a father figure, without a role model, without any help—spiritual help, or guidance to wrong and right. That wasn't there. So I went to church. Not the Lutheran; it was a little far from me. There was a nearby church called Monrovia for Pentecostals Church on 10th Street. I used to go there for Sunday school.

"[One day] when church was over, I was very sad. I was not in a good mood. This guy called Daniel Wallace, a member of the church, walked up to me and said, 'Hey, you don't look happy today. What's the problem?'

"He understood that I was not happy. He gave me some free time. I was still by myself in my aunt's house. Neighbor children were helping me. It didn't take that long—a week or so—when this guy insisted on actually seeing me, because he lived in the same community. And I decided to tell him what happened."

Daniel Wallace offered Semantics a place to live and food to eat, and began including him as part of the family.

Despite the help, Semantics was deeply depressed. He says that suicide is not common in Liberia, and is unacceptable. "But that's what I felt...I felt I wasn't of any use. I never told anybody, but those thoughts always came to my mind when I sat. That's why Daniel never allowed me to sit alone, you know—never. It even reached the point that his nieces became very jealous. I realized he was showing me much more love than the nieces. You know, whenever I saw him play with them, I would sort of imagine that this was how my dad used to play with me. And if he were around, he would have given me the same love, too."

Semantics soon became like a son to his new caregiver, who offered to help pay for his schooling if Semantics would sell shoes for him.

"So in the morning, I would take the shoes around Liberia's popular market in Monrovia, where people sell anything and everything. [Then] in the afternoon I would change into my uniform and go to school. The school had two sessions: they had a morning session and an afternoon session. So I opted for the afternoon session, and with that arrangement, I was able to complete high school.

Because he had to work, Semantics completed high school later than he normally would have. Immediately after graduating, he was offered a job at a radio station. "I didn't even apply for the job, I was just invited: 'Hey, come and join the team. We've been monitoring your reporting on high school radio!' But I needed to go to college. I told Daniel, and he offered the same arrangement: 'You can go to school, and then sell for me.' So I was about to enroll in the school of journalism.

"Many thoughts went through my mind. One thought that came into my mind and always remained with me is that I didn't need to take revenge with a gun to avenge the death of my dad—because I did want to join the rebel group. But my instincts told me that was not the best way—the best way to avenge the blood was to use the pen and my mouth. My voice.

"So I began working at the radio station. This has been my passion from five years old, you know. I told my dad I wanted to become a journalist. My mom said there were many questions I asked her while growing up and she had no answers, so I realized that in order to find the answers, I should become an interviewer."

When he graduated from high school and joined the radio station, Semantics moved back to Harbel. "It was a competent radio station established by the union workers of Firestone. I initially started as a newscaster, a reporter. But then I began to realize that I needed a platform, an audience that would be able to ask questions and perhaps find answers. The best way to do that was to formulate a program. I discussed that with my station manager, and he was like, 'Yeah, yeah, that's a brilliant idea.'

So from news casting I was promoted to programs, and I formulated my own talk show called *Others' Views*.

"It was about politics, human rights issues, labor issues, women's issues, education…many, many different issues. One time, I discussed an issue involving a worker at Firestone who was seriously injured with the machine he operated. The injury was not treated the way they should be, and I invited the labor secretary from Firestone to discuss the issue. And I invited the guy who was injured. I was questioning the morality behind what Firestone does, behind Firestone's slowness, their lackadaisical attitude in treating people. Because I advocated for that, and talked about it repeatedly, the injured man got better treatment.

This became his journalistic method. "So if you are accused of not doing something, I bring you and the person that accuses you in, and I would add my own opinion about what I think is the best thing to do.

"Given the fact that in Africa free speech is very expensive, I knew that I was taking a risk. But someone has got to take the risk, or someone has got to sacrifice. Someone has got to take the lead. I mean, if people didn't take the risk, we wouldn't have the United Nations, we wouldn't have rights organizations like Amnesty International! Even if it doesn't succeed, they will say 'He started that,' or, 'She started that.'

"I was at the radio station from 1998 until 2000. April 11th was the last day. Aside from *Others' Voices*, I had a night session on the air, which would play music and comment on social issues—relationship issues and things. Mondays, Wednesdays, and Fridays, from ten until midnight, I would be on air. So this night, I think it was a Wednesday night, I was on air. I signed off, and because we didn't have cars, we had to walk."

Semantics picks up a pen and looks around for paper, drawing a map of Harbel, which is divided into camps. He shows how he would commute into Camp 2, where the radio station was, across a bridge that divided the camps, and then draws a small road.

"I had signed off and began to walk on the smaller road," he says, "and I saw people seated at the end of the houses. I didn't know these were not normal people. I thought, 'Oh, Firestone workers.' I didn't know that these were people who had come for me.

"As I was walking, they jumped up and rushed at me and they were all, 'He's the guy! Let's get him!' And I was like, 'What have I done? What happened?' And they started beating me. They held my hands behind me, and one put their knife to me, saying if I refuse to go, they will cut. There were over five—I can't remember the exact number, but over five.

"I asked what happened, and one of them said, 'Our commander wants to see you.' I asked, 'Who's your commander?' But he just said, 'Well, if you get there, you will know the commander.'

"I was on my toes. I wouldn't walk normally. They held me up and they were forcing me to go and other things. I would have gone voluntarily if I wasn't tortured, if I wasn't beaten. I would have said, "Okay, so the commander wants to see me. Well let's go, let me get one or two presents and we'll go." But that wasn't the case, you know. So in the process of…of dragging me, beating me, we reached on the main road here. And they were just carrying me I didn't know where.

And we were approaching the bridge that divides Camp 1 and Camp 2. And then there's a beach right side of bridge. And so, as we were walking, from this end was a vehicle coming. And the lights were flashing. And so, when I saw the lights, they shoved me into this ditch. And one of them made a remark that if the car paused on the return, I wouldn't live to tell the story. And so, I was distressful. Very, unconscious, if you will. And then bleeding…you know, from my arm, from my nose, and…I said, 'Hold the car. Someone coming.' I muster up the courage, and thought that whoever that is in that car probably, if they are part of this group that didn't just kill me—I was going to go up on the road.

So I crawl on the main road and, um, knelt in the middle of the road as the car was approaching. So the cars stop and they jump out of their cars and they like, 'What's wrong with you, you crazy? Why are you in the middle of the road? Do you want to die?' and I said, 'Yes, I want to die.'

"And they're like, 'What happened?' And as they approached me, they saw me bleeding. So one of them cut a cloth, you know, from his trouser, plus he had to tie my hand to stop the bleeding and tied my head. And then I began to explain this, too…and them one of them said, 'Oh, but I know this guy! This is the guy that always talk on the radio right?' [The other said,] 'Oh yeah! I listen to his program!'

"They tied [up my wounds] and—and—and I told them, I said, 'Well, I didn't know what the thing that has happened.' And then they—they suggested that, 'Oh, look; the best thing for you to do is to leave this country now. Because it's not safe. Given what you experienced right now, it's not safe.'

And I said, 'Well, let's drive to Camp 1 so that I can pick up my belongings and whatever I have and then we go!' And they say 'No! If you want to go there, go alone. We won't go with you. Because we don't know...If they were there.' You know. So I said, 'Well, then, let's go.' I only had my press ID with me. I still have it today. The press ID. I still have it today."

Semantics was hidden between the front and back seats in the four-wheeled open-back jeep and was driven to the border with the Ivory Coast. He was able to convince the border guard that he was traveling on business and wanted to visit his family across the border. Since he only had his press ID with him, they believed him.

Semantics was twenty-one when he first went to the Ivory Coast. Rather than go to a refugee camp, Semantics got in a taxi not knowing where to go next. Semantics says the driver was a Liberian girl who took pity on him and offered him a place to stay—with her family.

"And then I told her what happened and her family was very, very generous to me. They opened up to me, but I wasn't happy. I had fears because one: language barrier—I couldn't speak French. Two: there was a mutiny in Abidjan at the time when Robert Guei was taking over and the rest of it, and so I was afraid and I didn't have documents to travel.

"If you don't have [the documents], they're going to arrest you. And so all those things and all the fears. I'm like, well this place is not safe for me, man. So I told my girlfriend—she eventually became my girl-friend—I told her, 'Well,' I said, 'Well, I've got to leave. I want to go.' She said, 'Where do you want to go?' I said, 'I want to go to Ghana! 'Cause Ghana...people there speak English, you know.'

"Through her help, we could put some money together for me and I boarded a bus and then I went to Ghana. I arrived in Ghana on August the 31st, 2000.

"I went there alone. And so I arrived there and went straight to the United Nation[s] offices and told them who I was and things and they said, 'Oh, yeah; your people are living [in] the camp so you can go there and meet your government.'

"So I went to the Refugee Warfare Council and told them that I came and I wanted a place to stay. And they said, 'Well, yeah; we have some places here where some people can go.' So I went to the room they showed me. But I wasn't happy, because, I mean, I was just there, and no one gives you food to eat. In fact, at the time, the UN refugee agency had withdrawn all direct support for the refugee camp, because they said that elections were held in Liberia in 1997 and Liberia has a president. So there was no support for Liberian refugees in Ghana, from 1997 until 2003. And imagine me arriving there at that time!

"But then, as I was there, Ghanaian media began to report issues about Liberian refugees that were not true. It didn't touch me, actually. But I was particularly touched about one incident when the *Ghanaian Chronicles* reported that Liberian refugees were being trained on the refugee camp to go and fight the war in Côte d'Ivoire. Without talking to authorities, without interviewing any refugees, they just wrote the story. The next day, Ghanaian military force moved onto us residents. In 2003. February 23rd. Moved on us with the military helicopters and guns and sniffer dogs looking for training places, looking for drugs, looking for whatever, around five in the morning. We were all forced to march on the scorching sun on the football field and taken around camp. It touched me. Only because of one reporter—someone did not investigate. So I said, well we got to do something. This is not true. And they searched. They didn't find one weapon. They did not see any drugs on people. They just humiliated us.

"And the international community—meaning the UN—this year was there, and did not say a word. I was touched, and I said, 'Well, I think we've got to do something. If we don't do it, people are going to ask why you did not do this when you saw a problem.' So I said, 'Well, I have to establish my own newspaper. I've got to counter some of the things [from] the Ghanaian media. And so I made a friend who became eventually my brother, you know. Not biological brother, very friendly. I told him, I said, 'Look, I've got these ideas. First I wanted to establish a radio station on the camp.'

"So I told the authorities in the camp. The government local representative was against that. They suppressed me. I couldn't get a radio station established in the camp. So I met a [Liberian] friend of mine who was a photojournalist who worked for a Ghanaian newspaper. So I talked to him. He's like, 'Oh, yeah! It's possible. I can show you the way through. In fact, what money do you have?' I said, 'I'm not working. I don't have money!' He's like, 'Well, I'll help with the money. You just deal with the stories and whatever.'

So it was set. We established the *Vision*. Before you run a newspaper in Ghana, you need to register it with government. So we went to the government regulate—the media regulatory body—and told them we wanted to run a newspaper. This purely refugee newspaper, nonprofit, just to get the refugees free. So, yeah, that was great!"

Semantics explains that the newspaper would be about refugees in the camps from many different countries.

"Because remember, a total number of forty-three thousand Liberians were in the [Buduburum] refugee camp. And I think aside from that number, there were about twenty-seven thousand who were indigenous people, who were Ghanaian people who were certainly in the refugee camp. And then, aside from that, there were also fifty thousand non-Liberians who were living there. Comprising of Ivorians, Nigerians, Togolese, Sudanese, Somalis, they were living there. So it's a huge community.

"So on May the 4th, 2004 we circulated our first edition of the *Vision* newspaper in the refugee camp. We ended up giving it to the refugees free because they're not paying it when we—when my friend uses money for us to publish the paper, we don't get the money back. You know."

So they applied for money from the United Nations to help fund their newspaper. "United Nations said they will get back to us. They are still getting back to us.

"We begin writing about issues that are of concern to the Liberian community and the refugee community in general. And so the bad atmosphere or relationship that existed between the host community—remember, the host community was very hostile to the refugees, you know. Because of...misconceptions. So the newspaper began to define who a refugee is, because many Ghanaians didn't know who a refugee is. They felt refugees are people who come and steal their wives, steal their women, took their money, took their jobs, and things. We began to explain circumstances that makes one a refugee and began to distribute the papers to people, to international organizations, to embassies—foreign embassies in that crowd. We gave them the papers freely.

"So we began to see the fruit—the impact that the paper was making. People in government circles began to look at a refugee from a different perspective. And they began to organize workshops for refugee leadership and inviting us, the media, to participate and keep talking about living together in peace, you know, as refugees and host people, you know.

"But eventually they say it shouldn't be called a 'camp'; it should be called a 'settlement,' because the resilience from the refugees transformed the refugee camp into a modern city where it had three Internet cafés, it had a level city, it had two banks, you know, and clocks, and bars...yeah.

"When the UN withdrew all direct support, most of the refugees had foreign support here. Families here would send them money and things. So they began doing their own businesses! Establishing schools for themselves! And people—refugee children—began to go to school, you know."

Semantics explains that the Ghanian government wanted to close down the newspaper for its criticism of the government, but they were not successful.

"And so the relationship between the two began to kind of be cooled because of what we were reporting, you know.

"I got in contact with a group in Canada called Journalists for Human Rights. It usually sends journalists—American, Canadian journalists—to

Africa to help discuss human rights issues. And the fact that it's all what the refugee newspaper was doing, about human rights, they were impressed. So seasonally they would send American journalists and student journalists from the US to go down and volunteer with us. One of them happened to come from the University of Chicago! And she was impressed. Among all of them, I give her the credit, because she paved the way for me to get the support that I needed for the newspaper. She went and asked me what I want. She said, 'I'm not rich. I don't have money. I'm a struggling graduate student, but what do you want? Tell me! Let's provide everything you want!' And then we began to put projects together and write. She was responsible for the newspaper to get its own website in 2005.

"We got a website, and as soon as people Google *Buduburum* it takes them to our website. And so people across the world began to read it [and say], 'Oh! This is amazing! Refugees have their own newspaper!' Liberians across the world were very proud in the Buduburum refugee camp because it's the only Liberian refugee camp that ever produced its own newspaper, in the world, you know.

"Even the UN this year had said it would help, and didn't do anything. When it was making report to Geneva office about projects and developments that refugees made in their host countries, I was shocked to see our website link on the UN this year! Our website! I was shocked! It improved, you know, to the extent that that website exposed us to the world. And people began coming, and as she left, she paved the way. More journalists went—more journalists from Columbia, from different universities, from Australia, from London...."

Semantics says that he met a British Israeli from London who ran an exchange program called Projects Abroad, which sends young college graduates to volunteer in Africa. After telling him about the newspaper project and explaining that they needed more money to publish it twice a month, the man offered to find him the funding. All he needed was four hundred dollars a month.

"We don't care for money. We only want the paper to be published for the people." And so he said, 'Well, I'm gonna do it.' And he began to publish, to pay that money for us to print the paper regularly.

"And so the world began to hear about us. And so, this day one of the journalists from Columbia University, Emily Polk, received a link from some of her friends at Columbia and the link spread out to friends and other people, and someone from the World Press Institute—based at Macalester, the World Press Institute. She went on the website and just emailed me: 'Hey Mr. Editor, given what you've done, we've got a program for international journalists. Would you mind telling us your experience, and would you mind coming over to America and come and see how press freedom works in America?'"

So Semantics applied to the World Press Institute. Out of two hundred applicants, Semantics was one of the ten selected for the program. "[There were applicants] from Brazil. From China. From Burma. From Spain. From Australia. From Senegal. From Papua New Guinea. And me from Liberia." So Semantics left the refugee camp and came to study at Macalester College in St. Paul.

Meanwhile, Semantics's mother back in Harbel, Liberia, found Semantics's contact information through a copy of his newspaper and a friend, who was also in Minnesota, had seen Semantics at her church.

"And so when the phone rings, at the other end was my mom. When she heard my voice, she was in tears. And I was in tears. And we began to explain to each other what happened and how. I thought they were dead. And she said, 'I had my son. My only son. He was dead. But now I've found him. He's not dead.'"

Semantics learned from his mother that he had a child—a daughter—with his former girlfriend. His daughter now lived with his mother. After applying for and receiving asylum in the United States, Semantics began the process to bring his daughter to the US through the Affidavit of Relationship immigration process.

Semantics says, "I started the process [for her to come to the United States]. She would want to come over, but the only concern she raised was that, 'Dad, if I come to you, what about my sister?' She's not my daughter! 'I cannot, yeah. Even with you—you will have to go through a DNA test and if the DNA doesn't match mine, the government is going to question if truly you're my daughter.' She's like, 'What? That DNA—no matter what it is—is going to prove that I'm your daughter. I'm a complete'—I mean, I'm just rephrasing this—'I'm a complete replica of you!'"

Today, Semantics is making a life in Minnesota, working at Target part time and going to school full time at Century College in White Bear Lake. He previously worked at the group home St. David's for Children, but needed to change jobs when he started school. After he finishes two years of community college, Semantics hopes to go to the University of Minnesota to study mass communication.

"I mean, this was my dream, to continue using the *Vision* in the refugee camp and then back in Liberia, to keep talking about human rights issues. That was my dream. I thought it would have continued, especially with me here."

However, Semantics soon learned that his team of refugee journalists in Ghana was no longer producing the paper because of a breakdown in leadership. "It frustrated me so much. So I said, well, the *Vision* is of course established exclusively for Liberian refugees in Ghana. And now that I'm in the US, I need to expand my scope of reporting. And I am just limited to refugees. So I changed that from the *Vision* to the *New Liberian*. *New Liberian*—to include all other people."

"I will forever be grateful of the United States government with all its criticisms and enemies across the world. I feel that United States still is a shining light on top of a hill. It gives hope to the hopeless. The Statue of Liberty that I visited in New York could be a sign of whatever they want. Maybe a sign of freedom. But for me, the Statue of Liberty is not just a sign of freedom. It is life for me. It means life. Not death. And so, I consider the generosity that the United States offers people like me. And I'm much more appreciative of that, despite the fact that it is a human country governed by human beings—imperfect human beings—there isn't any utopia on this planet. But in many ways, United States, it's apart from other countries. Not least as exemplified by what just recently transpired by Barack Obama becoming president.

"And so I really, really appreciate the US government for granting me asylum. It has been doing that for generations, even before me. And I believe its citizens have got to hold on to what they have. You know, because others may not have it, and because they don't have it, they might become jealous or envious of it, and they would like to destroy that which the United States has. So with all its problems, with all its human imperfections, it's important that Americans realize that they have something very, very good. And they should preserve that which they have, because if they lose track of that, they may not get it. They may not have any place afterward to call home. Because no country is going to accept them as refugees if there is a civil war here!

"And I might also add that the family unit needs to be held together in America. The American family is struggling. Very, very much struggling. And I think that the government needs to do things, devise strategies, mechanisms; because the stronger families make strong nations. If families are not strong, countries don't become strong. And so, it should do whatever it can to make families remain uniting units in the United States."

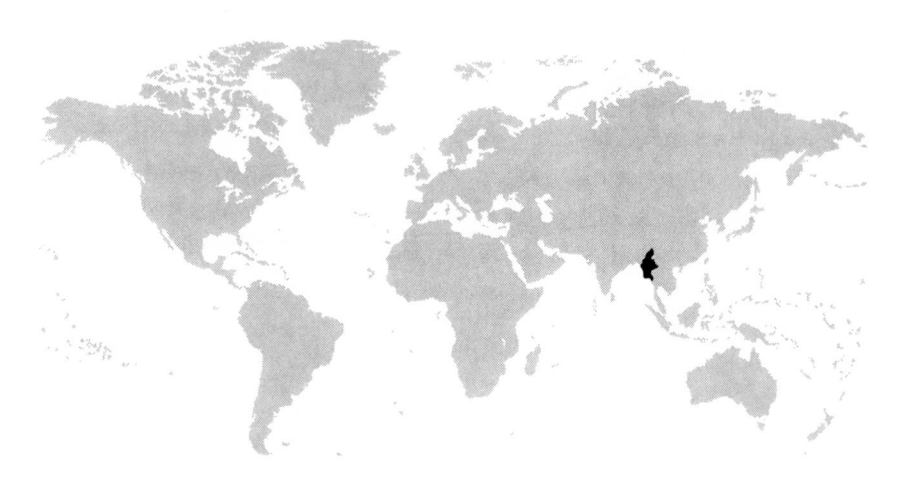

Burma (Myanmar)

Despite the fact that Burma's[21] independence from Britain was granted peacefully in 1948, Burma has experienced significant internal unrest based on colonial-era loyalties, cultural and religious differences, and different views of how the country should be governed. These tensions have been exacerbated by extreme poverty in Burma and the presence of a repressive government with few transfers of power since Burma's independence.[22] [23] Since 1990, Burma's military government, the State Peace and Development Council, has violently persecuted ethnic minorities.[24]

The UNHCR reports that over 490 thousand refugees—mostly the Karen, Karenni, and Chin—have fled Burma, and most reside in refugee

---

21. Until recent decades the international community called the country *Burma*—the informal name for the country in Burmese is *Bamar*. In 1989 the military government requested foreigners to only refer to the country as *Myanmar*, the linguistically more formal name. Many international businesses and organizations such as the United Nations have adopted this new name without reservation, but many persist in using Burma as the name for the country for a variety of reasons including opposition to the ruling military government. MCC Refugee Services has chosen to continue to refer to the country as Burma because, in general, it is the accepted name used by the Karen refugees resettled in Minnesota.

22. Church World Service, "Karen Refugees."

23. Nobelprize.org, "Aung San Suu Kyi: Biography."

24. Church World Service, "Karen Refugees."

camps in neighboring Thailand.[25] The two countries have similar tropical monsoon climates with rainy, humid summers and dry, mild winters.[26]

Over two thousand Karen refugees have resettled in Minnesota, coming in large numbers since 2004.[27] The Karen are an ethnic group indigenous to southeast Burma. The Karen primarily practice Christianity or Buddhism, and they speak the Karen language. Additionally, some Karen people are able to speak the national language, Burmese.

25. UNHCR.org, "Myanmar."

26. CIA World Factbook, "Burma."

27. Minnesota Department of Health, "Primary Refugee Arrivals to Minnesota."

Kaw Lah:
Goal Setter, Human Being

Twenty-seven-year-old Kaw Lah has been in Minnesota for just a few weeks when he tells his story in a small room at Minnesota Council of Churches offices. He keeps his light blue Colombia jacket and his backpack on the entire time. Most of his long hair is tied back in a ponytail. Kaw Lah is worried about not being able to represent the Karen people well or fully enough, but wants the story of the Karen to be heard. He was born in Burma, the Karen state, in 1981.

"I remember one thing: when we ran into the cliffs," he says, "we ran into the cliffs because the government troops were coming. When military troops came to attack our villages, we had to run away. During that time I was five, maybe six years old. I just knew we were not eating or playing. The old people would say, 'We have to go,' and we would go and sleep in the cliffs. We could not study during that time. Some days, the teacher told me, 'Today you cannot come because the situation is not good.'" As a child, Kaw Lah only understood this: "We were fleeing something."

Running to the cliffs was frequently necessary at that time, and daily life was not the same there. "The old people told me, 'Keep quiet. We have to keep silent, because…'" he pauses. "You know what *piyo* means?" he asks. "During that time we called the Burmese *piyo*. And when the old people say, '*Piyo* is coming!' We have to keep silence. We were afraid of *piyo*." The group would return after a few days.

"When I was five or six years, maybe four or five years old, we moved because of too much military troop activity in my village area. We mov to the taller mountain to find a safe place. But one year later, the military troop activity expanded to there, too.

"During that time, my father was caught—we can say arrested. We didn't know when he would return...we waited and we waited. I was the only child in my family." Kaw Lah waited with his mother. "The military troops arrest the Karen because they need more porters to carry the food for the military.

"When the Burmese army was attacking it was really hard to explain that we are not the KNU[28]. If we mention we are not KNU, they continue arresting anyway because they need more porters. If people don't want to go, you have to pay money, but as you know, we are living like..." Kaw Lah stops to explain, "We have not seen money before. Normally, the main career that people do is croppings—growing rice. Most people farm, and sometimes we raise the animals. The piyo do not provide anything for the porter, and they discriminate against the Karen people like animals, so the porters run away.

"My father and his friend tried to run away. The Burma military—the soldiers—tried to arrest them back. And the shooting...the target that they shot was my father. All I know is that my father was shot by the *piyo*."

Kaw Lah describes what happened after his father's arrest. "We were waiting. We were waiting, but I didn't know what is going on. I didn't quite understand, but maybe the old people didn't tell me anything. My mother's face was not well, like she felt sad, something like that, and after one year or two years, she got sick. She passed away after two years from illness, maybe disease. Other people told me she had malaria, attacking the brain or something like that. I don't quite understand. But I still had my grandma.

"We didn't want to live in the refugee camps, but we had no choice to stay in Burma. Village after village was attacked. My grandmother and I took a boat. You know the Salween River? Salween River is a big river,

---

28. The Karen National Union, the mainstream rebel movement fighting for autonomy for the Karen state from Burma (Myanmar).

and we took a boat across it from Rata to Ee Htu Hta, on the border between Thailand and Burma.

"I did not really go to school yet during that time because, you know, we kept moving. Well, I went to school, but it was not normal, because we had to move, always move, move. I was eight years old after we crossed the river. We stayed in a temporary resettlement place, a place with tents and small buildings. It was quite small, and the Thai soldiers make sure the people stay there: you can't leave. During that time, the Thai Burma Border Consortium provider supplied some shelter and clothes.

"We later moved into Thailand, to Mekong Ka Refugee Camp. This refugee camp is quite permanent, and I was there maybe seventeen years. I started my education properly. I graduated high school.

"We had good support from the NGOs. The building construction in the refugee camp was better than other countries like Ethiopia, or Kenya, or something like that, I have heard—not my imagination. As I understand and I *do* feel, we are good, we had better support, more than other country. And…I do believe it is somewhat because most of the Karen people are Christian.

"We believe in the *Pgho*[29]," he says. "We believe in the traditional, believe in the forest. I grew up in that kind of family. But later on, when I stayed with my grandma who is Christian, I became Christian automatically. In the camps there are lots of Christians, many, many churches. I am in the Karen Christian community. If you ask someone, 'Do you believe pgho?' You may say no. I do believe, but I don't want to say something like that. But I did not realize what I believe. I should move somewhere to have a better place to—better things to—believe something in."

In the camps, Kaw Lah began to teach with the Karen education project and ZOA Refugee Care.[30]

After teaching, Kaw Lah became a field officer for ZOA Refugee Care

---

29. According to traditional Karen belief, pgho is the term for a certain impersonal force that cannot be overcome, but can reside in individuals to give them power.

30. ZOA Refugee Care is a Dutch international relief and rehabilitation organization that is dedicated to assisting people affected by armed conflict and natural disasters. It supports refugees, internally displaced persons (IDPs), returnees, and others in their transition to stability.

for about five years, working on supply distribution and writing field reports. Then he was given a chance to resettle.

"The first time I got an opportunity to resettle in Norway. But I did not feel confident; I think, 'Oh, I don't want to go.' So I answered my grandma, 'No, I prefer to stay in Thailand. I can look after myself.' So she said 'Okay, not a problem; sure.' She went. After one year alone I think 'Oh! What is going on?'

"My understanding of the US was...what is the big, what is the best, what is the good, what is the challenge? I think the most powerful country in the world is the US. And the process is easy and fast. I couldn't wait for Australia. The young people are encouraged to come here to the US to find a new world and for the challenge.

"I was not scared. I was confident to come. I believe that I can progress, can arrive at my ambitions. When we are working in the community, we are happy. One of the foreign teachers in the camp said, 'It is good to travel and to collect everything. You want to know, you want to taste, you want to touch, you have to go. If you don't go, you cannot learn anything. You have to challenge yourself.' I got this encouragement, and also I want to have a degree. I want to study. I don't want the time to pass away for nothing. I want to be active. I want to go. I don't want to stay at home and sleep and eat.

"At the first training provided by IOM [the International Office of Migration], one of the trainers asked, 'What do you want to be?' I said I want to be secretary of the United Nations; I like Kofi Annan." Kaw Lah laughs.

"Before I came, I communicated with other Karen who had come to Minnesota. I asked them, 'How is life?' They answered, 'Oh, not well yet; it is hard. And there are a lot of strong hurricanes [snowstorms]...I thought, *Is not safe for me!* But I decided to come."

When he arrived, Kaw Lah was lucky enough to speak English fairly well; he had studied in school in the camp. He says, "I have no idea to go back. Yes, we should list now what we want to do: I want to see snow. Soon that will be completed—then I have to complete another thing: education. I have to work. I want to have a house. Yes, I have many plans.

But normally, I have no idea to go back. Although it is very cold, and I walk outside for a few minutes and I think, *Oh, am I wrong to go here!* But I am still here."

Kaw Lah ends with one last thought about leaving the camp where he had spent seventeen years of his life. "The one thing that I try to tell everybody I was leaving was just know what you are, be yourself. One thing I have to know is that I am Karen. I don't want to show off that my culture is good, but some of my country is very nice. We have to be proud that we are one of the ethnic groups that is given from God.

"I just know that I am a human; I have to know myself, where we come from. Everyone can live together in peace. To be proud to be Karen is good, but we are proud that we are one of the nationality, we aren't proud to be biggest of nationality. We are happy with peace, and working."

Lah Paw:
Community Gardner, Eager Learner

Lah Paw, a Karen woman from Burma, tells her story in her apartment on the east side of St. Paul. She sits on the floor, on a large straw mat covering the carpet. She holds her baby in her lap as her older two-year-old daughter plays with a neighbor girl. Lah Paw tries to shoo them into the other room to keep the noise down, but their shrieks and chattering still pierce the air. Lah Paw was not resettled through MCC Refugee Services, but she rose up as a leader in her apartment complex's community garden, which was organized by MCC and some MCC volunteers. Lah Paw speaks English well enough to communicate, but she finds it difficult to tell her story in what, to her, is a foreign language. Nevertheless, Lah Paw is cheerful and calm as she relates the details of her life. She sits with her legs crossed under her Karen dress; it is embroidered with traditional Karen designs and colors.

"My name is Lah Paw. You want to know my age, too? I'm twenty-eight years old. I'm from Burma. I was born in Burma, but when I was nine years old, I became a refugee. I lived in a small village—yes, a small village in the mountains. Yes. We have thirty houses in the village. People in the village, including my mother and father, are all farmers. They grow plants and rice. And vegetables.

"When I'm in the village, I have go to school. But it is very difficult to find the teacher and then the villagers, we have to pay the teacher like three...how can I say it in English? We have no money to pay the teacher, so we will give teacher rice. A hundred fifty pounds per year. For each child." Lah Paw laughs, a bright, airy kind of laughter. "Something like that."

"Yes, I have one brother and one sister. I'm youngest. When I'm three years old, my father was dying. But I continue to go like this. My mother have us, but my brother and sister can't go to school, because my father dies and the...they are...how can I say? Like not slaves. They go to another person's house and the rich men give the price and then some money. [They] clean house and they go to the farm. They do the planting and farming."

Lah Paw explains that her brother and sister lived where they worked, but came to visit her at least once a month. She stayed home because she was the smallest, she says.

"I went to school. Just like ABCD." Lah Paw laughs again, as though at herself. "But when I'm nine years old, it was difficult for...for food. Sometimes the Burmese soldiers came to our village and then they catch the pig or hen or animal that they want and they kill them and then they eat. Sometimes they fight with the Karen soldiers and then my mom is very afraid about that.

"After that, my sister was seventeen or near eighteen and she got married. Yes. My older sister and her husband." Lah Paw points up to the wall where several family pictures are hanging. There is a picture of a Karen woman and man in traditional Karen dress, as well as a man in a dark shirt and woman in a white dress.

"The wedding picture is me, but the white one [is her]. Yes. And then she got married with the refugee man. My sister's husband is already in the refugee camp. He wanted to know about the villagers in Burma. He went to visit and he saw my sister and then he asked for my mom and then they got married. And after that I follow them to the camp."

This was good timing, Lah Paw explains, because it was becoming increasingly unsafe to remain in the village.

"It was not safe. Not safe. Two, three times a month we needed to run and sleep, sleep outside the village. Sometimes we run in the forest and then we sleep there. Sometimes near the river. Yes. No, no house—how can I say? No camp. Not easy."

Lah Paw says her mother came too, but was experiencing a disability.

"She is already here. But now she has not ability. She is one of the disability people now. She probably is, uh, drop, drop—I can't call it in English." Lah Paw clears her throat, trying to explain. "She can't speak very well, can't walk very well. And she cries and laughs. Sometimes when she sees new people and they seem happy, then she cries. When she feels sad she cries. Sometimes when she is sad, she smiles. How can I say? I don't know." Lah Paw gives up, laughing. "She became disability people. My sister take care of her. Yes. My sister's husband died in the camp."

Lah Paw lived in more than one camp on the Thai-Burmese border. "The first camp for me is Sho Klo and then...I lived there five years and then I moved to another camp, the Mae La camp. How many years?" Lah Paw laughs, trying to remember. "Fourteen years."

Lah Paw grew up in the camp and went to a school called Number One High School. One of her former teachers is now a case manager at MCC Refugee Services.

"He is my principal. He's my teacher. He teach me science. But maybe he thinks he can't memorize me because there were so many students." Lah Paw laughs again.

She explains that as a small child, she, like many other child refugees, did not realize exactly why they were living in the camp. "But when I'm grown, I'm bigger and then I know, oh, I'm a refugee because we—we are in the camp. I can go to school and there I have a food enough, but we can't go outside. We have to stay in the camp. There are Thai soldiers or Thai police around our camp and then we can't go outside. We just stay in the camp. Sometime we feel sad."

There were happy times, too—like when she met her husband.

"My husband, we are the same camp, *but* we are in different sections. Yes. I'm in Zone C he is in Zone A. After I graduated high school, and then I continue to...I want to learn more about English, so I went to the Bible School that was taught in English. Theology was very, very difficult for me. I can't graduate from that school, but I have a little more English. Then when we are Bible school students, we had to go to another church to teach Sunday school one week at a time. I went to the Zone A. My husband, yes, his uncle is the pastor in the Hosanna Church. I go to the church and then teach Sunday school." Lah Paw laughs.

Lah Paw goes on to explain the protocol surrounding a Christian marriage in her culture.

"Before we get to marry, we are just lovers. And then we decided we would get married, so we told the pastor at my own church. At his own church, and for our culture, before we get married, we can have no *sex*." She says the word emphatically. "No sex. After getting married, it's okay. Before getting married the pastor asks us—how can I say?—are you clean in your man and lady relationship? We said yes. And then we got married in the church.

"We make the paper invitations to give to our friends. And then many people came to our wedding. [There is a] big celebration and after that...we are married in the morning and then we have breakfast after."

Lah Paw's mother was able to celebrate, too.

"She was happy and she cried a lot," she says with laughter. "My mother-in-law and my father-in-law are in Burma. They are in Rangoon. But my mother-in-law, she came to my wedding."

"When I am single, always I'm in the school, and then when after I get married, I worked. I had a job like, uh...I will breastfeed? Is okay if I...?" Lah Paw gestures to the baby on her lap and begins to nurse, unashamed.

As her baby nurses, Lah Paw explains that she worked at a clinic in the camp where she counseled pregnant women about HIV.

"When pregnant women come to the clinic, I teach them about how they can protect themselves from HIV and how you can get HIV. After that I take one or two cc's of blood. Then...how can I say?" Lah Paw pauses, trying to find the words. She explains that she sent the blood away for testing, and then met with the women again when they came back for the results.

"The ones who have HIV, we test again to be sure. And then the women who have HIV when they are pregnant seven months, the doctor give them medicine to protect the baby. The mom already have, but because of the protected medicine, the baby doesn't have the HIV." She laughs again, because she is having difficulty explaining. "In my language it is very, very easy to say but in English...it is very hard to explain about that.

"I feed my baby and I will tell you about the breastfeeding. In the Karen people, when we are at the camp, no problem about breastfeeding in front of the people or men, but when I came here, very different." Lah Paw laughs again as she shrugs.

"When we go cleaning or offsite we need to cover something and then sometimes...I pump my breast and I put it in the bottle," she says, laughing again. "But in my apartment, no problem.

"I have one teacher who was from America, from what state I can't remember. His name is Karl. When he is in the camp, many ladies will take showers outside in the river and then we wear this one here"—Lah Paw pantomimes tying a long piece of cloth around herself, secured under her arms—"and then we take the water in the cup and then we shower like that." She pantomimes pouring water over herself. "And there he said, 'I feel shy.'" She laughs. "'Why you feel shy, teacher?' I asked him. 'Oh, I never saw before like this!'" Lah Paw laughs at the memory.

"But here, people can't take baths outside just...in village we don't have it like this! Yes, here is easy because the big city...but very expensive.

"Sometimes I miss my; I miss my camp. We are here, and many of our problems are gone. We never saw snow before we came here. But before I came here, when I saw snow in the video—oh, I very like! And then"—Lah Paw pauses and chuckles—"I want to see and I want to touch. And then when I came here, 'Uh oh; no more. Go away!'" She laughs animatedly. "Very cooold. I never had asthma, but when I came here, now I have asthma. I won't take the bus outside sometime. We don't have coats for snow time."

Lah Paw arrived in Minnesota in July 2008, joining her brother. She explains that when they decided to apply for resettlement, they first applied to other countries.

"My husband and I, we have opportunity now. We can come to the big country like this. Australia, Canada, Norway, Sweden, America; America is very easy. So before I applied to America, I applied to Australia. But no one call us. And then I come back to America. Applying to America is direct. Yes." She says that it was harder for her husband to leave because his entire family was still living in Burma, but they knew they would have better opportunities for jobs and education if they came to America. She took some English classes when she first arrived, but when her baby was born, she stopped. She says she hopes to continue her education, maybe even get her GED, when her baby is bigger.

"I decided by myself. And then I...um, my doctor told me that if I try, I could become a good interpreter." Laughing, she continues. "'Good doctor, *no* good doctor,' I said. But interpreter is...I'll try. Yes, we see something like that. We see school for our baby, too. And then they will get the good school and the good education."

Lah Paw and her family were not resettled through MCC, but their first experiences were similar to other refugees like them. She remembers back to her first moments in America.

"I'm very, very excited. And that this is the first time before we have experiences we saw the movie and the video.[31] I worry about that. And then if I—how can I say?—when I'm in the airport, how can I use the restroom? I have never seen a nice restroom like this. So how can I use that? But my husband grew up in Rangoon, the big city. Yes. And then I told—I told him, 'Before I go to the restroom, you go first and then come back and then tell me if I can do it.' Yes, he helped me," Lah Paw says, laughing at the memory. "In the in airplane he also helped me, too."

Another new thing for her was the housing situation in the United States.

"In Burma, we build our homes by ourselves. The poor person, we make our house, we build our house with bamboo. The rich man's house is made of wood. And then one, two, or three years we fix [our houses]. We don't need to buy much like this. This is different. But when we came here, if we don't have a job and then sometime we have enough food, but we worry...we worry about the rent for apartment.

---

31. During their predeparture cultural orientation given by the International Office of Migration, many refugees watch a video about what to expect in their new lives in the United States.

"Some people, they are—they are new, so the government gives them cash for rent for their apartment, but it is not enough. It's not easy. And then sometime we miss our small house." She laughs. "Yes. That was our own, yes. Here not by—how can I say?—not owned by myself. We pay and then when we don't have money, we go outside. Something like that. But in Burma, in the camp, it is small, it is bamboo, but it is our own, so don't worry about that."

Lah Paw now begins to speak about her involvement with the community garden in her neighborhood and what it means for her neighbors from Burma.

"When we are in the camp we grow some plants. If you want to grow, you need to pay twenty *baht* in the Thai money. Twenty baht or thirty or fifty depending on the...depending on the..." She laughs. "I don't know how to say it. But if you don't have money you can grow and then buy, day by day...something like that. Yes. I never thought about gardening when I'm in America. Before I came here, some people in the camp told me that if you go to America—no...no...work—how can I say? No, grass. There is no grass, just buildings and the big buildings, tall buildings. I say, 'Really?' So I never think about a garden. But when I'm in Illinois, no garden for me. But when I'm in Minnesota, I saw the meeting about the garden; that is the first time since we are here that the Karen people in my apartment complex, we feel very, very happy." She smiles, laughing contently. "Yes, a small garden, but we feel like we are in our country. Yes, in the summertime."

Fifteen Karen families, a Nigerian family, and an American family living in the complex developed the community garden, with the support of MCC Refugee Services, local volunteers, donors, and the property owners. Together, they cultivated their garden. Lah Paw explains that they grew pumpkins, corn, peas, carrots, and other vegetables specific to Burma and Thailand—then they sell them at the farmer's market. The garden has also become a place to make new friends.

"Before we are here, we had come from different camps. But we don't know the other people; we just stay in the room. But in the summertime, we go outside. 'Oh I want to plant too, too, too,'" Lah Paw says, her voice getting higher as she describes the excitement surrounding the garden. She tells of the questions neighbors asked one another when they began talking to each other: "'Where are you from? Where are you staying? Are you plant this? Good!' And then we look and we have a new friend. That's great!"

Lah Paw's husband works with vegetables too, but at Bix Produce Company. She says it is close and an easy job, but she thinks she will also need to start working when her baby is bigger.

"Because my husband makes not even seven dollars per hour. Seven dollars and eighty cents per hour, and then not eighty hour per week. No—just only sometime sixty hours, sometime seventy. So it is not enough. Seven hundred dollars for rent per month. It is not easy." Still, she laughs. "So I hope—I hope I will get a better job. And then I will go to school, too, and then when I become a—I will try to become an America citizen. Then, if I have a good time, I will go and visit in Thailand. Then my husband decided when he becomes a citizen and have a good job, and when we have saved some money, then maybe I think we go back to stay in the Thailand. But my kids are here and continue to go to school. Yeah. We will go back and come back, like something like that."

Lah Paw pauses for several seconds, the silence hanging comfortably around her.

"Yes, for me, wintertime is not easy. When I breathe the snow, the cold, I need to put the air…" she pantomimes using an inhaler, laughing at the same time.

She goes on now to say what she wants Minnesotans to know about the Karen.

"I would like to tell about Karen people, refugees from Burma. We are the good person. We all have kindness. And we need the American people's love and their kindness, to welcome us.

"I have an experience. I go outside and then I see—I see a black person. I don't know if he is good or bad. He asked me, 'Are you Hmong or Karen?' I say, 'I'm Karen.' [He said,] 'Please give me seventeen dollars. Because I have face a big problem. I'm from California. I'm a new person in Minnesota. I don't know about the Minnesota situation. I don't have any more gas. I'm in the American army.' He shows me his ID. I don't know what I say, but I throw away the garbage I had with me. I don't have seventeen dollars in my hands, but I told my sister, 'Give me twenty dollars and then I will give him.' And then my sister—my sister can't speak English—and then she give me twenty dollar and then I give him. I feel like he already know Karen people easy to give." She laughs. "Maybe he know about that before he asked. Before he asked for money he asked me, 'Are you Hmong or are you Karen?'" She laughs some more. "When we are in the village or in Burma, if we see the people who have problems and then we help them always, but every country, every village, every nation, have the good and bad. Do you know what I mean?

"I want to say our Karen people, we have the…we have the good behavior. To help people, love other people." Lah Paw explains that the Karen people now need Minnesotans' help. "If you see the Karen people, you already know the difference."

Lah Paw says she is thankful she was asked to tell her refugee story. "But many families have a different history. Yes. But I have opportunity to tell about my story like this, so I tell you. Thank you."

Josiah:
Pastor, Community Leader

Josiah is a case manager at MCC Refugee Services when he tells his story early one October morning. He smiles often and laughs easily.

Josiah begins his story with his parents. "My dad was working with the British government before the Second World War and my mom was a nurse in the hospital." During WWII, the Karen supported the British armed forces in Burma."

"My earliest childhood memory is that I dreamed of going to the far country. This is my early child dream because like I would love to go to...let me say, a white country. You know what I mean? White country doesn't mean just America. Any country for white people—England, Australia, America, whatever. Because I liked the Western culture, and the Western dress.

"[In] 1967 or 1968, we were arrested by the Burmese government. I was two years old. My father was in the countryside, with the KNU revolutions; he was in the army. The Burmese government actually tried to look for my dad, but they could not get him, so they detained my mom and us.

"We were in the prison a year, but I was a child, I did not know anything. After my brother and I were released, [my mom] was still in prison for seven years. After seven years, she was released, but she was under house arrest and could not work. Under house arrest she is to stay at home; she can't travel. We were supported by my mom's sister and brother, and my father [secretly] supported us sometimes. He was not running from the government, but he was in the revolution area fighting for the democracy and freedom. The Burmese government could not search him because they had their army in the Karen state. It's like a fence: we can't cross to them and they cannot come to the city and meet their families.

"My mother was under house arrest for five years. She was not allowed to go anywhere and she had report to the military government every month. Me and my brother, we grew up with our aunt and uncle, my mother's siblings. We continued our education and after I graduated, my mom told me that [to] get a job would be pretty hard, because my dad was involved with the revolutions. Even [when] I was applying for the government assistance in my college, they did not grant it because of my dad.

"I graduated at the University of Rangoon [with a] bachelor's in Economics. For me and brother, there is no problem; we could go to school freely, but we could not get any financial aid or any assistance from the government because of my dad's involvement with the revolution. In the meantime, my mother is willing to join my dad in a family reunion after the seventeen years separation."

His parents had not communicated during those long years and Josiah explains why. "If the government knew that you had connection with your husband, they would put you back in prison, right back in jail. Because out of house arrest they are under watch, back and forth, and if you have connection with your husband, they would put you [back in jail]. And you would not be able to communicate with anyone else.

"She wanted to reunite with my dad. We just call my dad a spy for KNU, one of the leaders of the KNU. One day, my dad sent his man to take us to the border, to the revolution area, so my mom decided to follow then. Me and my brother [also went], we left Burma and we moved to the Thai-Burmese border, which is a KNU-controlled area to the family reunion."

At this point, Josiah was twenty-two. He had not seen his father since he was five years old. "We did reunite with him, but he doesn't recognize us. We did not know him." Josiah laughs. "But he was so kind to his family after we reunited with him. After five years he passed away. He passed away from illness. So we had a chance, an opportunity for five years with him after our family reunion.

"After we arrived at the Thai-Burmese border, I started to learn the Thai language and six months [after] that I went to Thai seminary. I was born from the Christian family. [My father] grew up from the Buddhist family and after he married my mom, he converted to Christian. My mother was a very strong Baptist. Since I was a child, every Sunday I had to go to the Sunday school class and go to the church, so we got a very good foundation and base faith in the family. It has built our lives till now. We have this Christian faith still."

As a child, Josiah hadn't expected that he'd attend seminary. "Obviously, I did not expect to go to the seminary because I wanted to become a lawyer. I never thought I would go to a seminary. But in Thailand, I did not have any future; [this was] the only way to get education. In Karen, we have the Baptist alliance connection. One of my pastors from the Thai–Burmese border, in the revolution area, connected me with Thai churches in Thailand and I got the opportunity to attend the seminary.

"Obviously, I was not a proper read person because I haven't finished my education in Thailand and as well I didn't know much Thai language. I couldn't read or write, but I started to learn. I spent two years in the seminary. Actually, after I graduated, I could speak fluent Thai. I know Thai very well—read or write.

"[Then] I had the mission team which is called the Asian Tribal Ministries in Thailand. I worked with the Asian Tribal Ministries [for] two years in the northern part of Thailand. We evangelized to the tribal people. I am working for the logistician and the training center for development.

"After that, I got married. My wife she was a teacher in the Karen state. Her family and my family are very close friends, so I didn't realize I will marry with her, but I don't know, this is God's plan." Josiah laughs. "We dated, and in 1988 I got married with her. I got married in Thailand and I quit the Asian Tribal Ministries. I got a job with Médecins Sans Frontières.[32] I was working [in an] administrator position. I worked there

---

32. Doctors Without Borders (French).

for seven years, at the Thai-Burmese Border. I lived in the city. The office is located in Mae Sot[33] and we provided medical supplies to the camp every day and with the nurses and doctors from overseas.

"My wife worked a year. After she quit, she is living with me in the city and she doesn't work; she is a housewife." Josiah and his wife, Daisy, have three children. "They all are born in Thailand…all my children's names are given by my mom.

"My given name is Josiah, but I don't want to take and keep my father's name, because my father's name is a little bit traditional name; it will be hard to spell. So I submitted my documents and applied just to keep my name Josiah as a last name, and my first name become Saw." In the Karen language, *saw* means mister, a fact Josiah often tells with a big grin stretched across his face.

"After [working with Médecins Sans Frontières] I switched to another job. My position is program manager with Handicap International. In 1999, I got the management training in Lyon in France [for] six months, and then I came back to Thailand, and then after that, in 2000, I came to US.

"When I first came to the US, I planned to pursue my education. I didn't get the student visa. I got my visa for ten years because I was working with the NGO; they issued me a long visa to travel around the world. I hold the Thai documents when I came to the US. My wife [doesn't] have any status in Thailand. Even my children, born in Thailand, don't have any legal status. Even my status is somewhat fake…you know fake status? I bought some documents. Just for survival," he laughs. "Because obviously, I am not Thai. I am originally from Karen, from Burma, so it's against the law. But you can pay bribes, you know. You can get your status when you have money. You need to know the language very well. And that is my situation—I got everything. But my family, they don't have any status.

"After I came here, I submitted my asylum. First I came to California. I have distant relatives there, and I visit and live with them. I spent a few months there and [then] I moved to Colorado. To get the job there. I worked with friends at a sushi bar. During the time, I submitted my

---

33. A Thai town that borders Burma.

asylum. Later on, I tried to apply for my family to be here." Josiah's family reunification process took two and half years.

"After I was granted my asylum, I travelled to the East Coast...Texas, Chicago, Wisconsin, looking for somewhere...I moved to Minnesota. In 2003, a huge number of Karens came to Minnesota and a bunch of my friends invited me to come and have a look here. But at first I didn't like it, because of the weather for humanity. I liked the Colorado weather. And then I decided to go back to Colorado, but they said, 'Oh, you should live here. You can find a job here. You know, even the weather is not a big deal.' I said, 'Okay, let's try.' So the end of 2003, I was here.

"I started working with in July 2004. My family arrived in August. My oldest daughter, she was sixteen, fifteen years old, and she started the ninth grade. My son, he came to eighth grade, he was thirteen, and my youngest daughter started with the fifth grade.

"In Thailand, they attended a private school, so they knew a lot of English before they came to US. We planned it before I came here, so that they learned in the private school and after they came here it was not so difficult for them. In just six months, they know everything—yes."

Josiah says he is not worried about his children losing touch with the Karen language or culture. "Many of the older generation are concerned, but myself I don't keep serious for this point. Like American history, when you go back, people came from the Europe maybe two, three, four, five generations ago, they lost their native language, you know. Maybe you are from Norwegian, German, or French origin. So I know that this is going to be happening definitely. In three or four generations, maybe no more Karen; they are going to become American.

"I expect that, so I don't take it serious...I don't feel any serious for this part. But my parents' generation—in the community you will see [that the] old generation, they keep very serious for that. However, American is American. Your face is probably like the Asian face, but you will speak just English. You will know only the American culture; the culture will be changed completely. Even though you will want to control, maybe you can do, just a little bit, maybe less, but they will completely change to US culture, I guess.

"After I come here, my mom passed away on 2005. I tried to reunite with her, but my mom doesn't want to come to US. She says, 'You go. I don't want to go, because I am old, I want to live in my land, my homeland.'" Josiah laughs. "It's pretty hard for the old people. In 2005 January, she was passed away. My brother is still there. He is planning to go to England."

"I don't think I am [going] back to Burma unless the government changes. I don't think I will move back there. I don't have anything there. I don't know people there. But if the situation changes [in Burma], I wish to visit sometime.

"I wish to go back to Thailand. Because my adult life I grew up in Thailand. But I don't want to set up my life there—just to visit, maybe three months. Before, we are the displaced, and displaced people have no legal status. So now we are so glad to be living in America and get the legal status. We can legally live the center of our lives here, so we are very glad."

"Obviously, [being an] asylee is a little bit hard, when or before you submit your documents and you declare yourself to US government. But after I worked with the refugees program here, I do understand that we are not different. Asylees and refugees are the same: we have equal opportunity."

Josiah will apply for his citizenship in the coming year. He doesn't worry about becoming too much of an American or losing touch with the Karen culture. "I don't feel for this point much. [I] am a little bit strange in my family's life. My dad was very active with the Karen revolution, freedom, and democracy. My mind is very strong in the faith, the Christian faith. I never wear my Karen dress. Since I was a child, I liked Western culture. I like to wear the pants, shoes, tie, and suit. So [I] am so strange to the family...my mom taught me, 'Oh, you are Karen. You are to remember where you came from,' you know. But my brother is just fine, he is flexible.

"When I came to the US, I am so glad. And even Thailand, Thailand dress is like the Western dress, so [I] am so happy. I had seen movies since I was a child; I liked the dress and the culture. When I was a child we all watch the James Bond. James Bond movies. I know who is the actor, the first James Bond is Sean Connery, after that Roger Moore, and the third one is Timothy Dalton, and then, now is…now I forgot his name. Daniel Craig. Yes, that's right. Yes, action films I like.

"To maintain the culture, I will say one [necessary thing] is the dressing, and another one is your behavior and your feeling. In our Asian and Karen culture, we respect the older people. We call them mom, dad, uncle, aunt something like that. We don't call their names, like Mike. Another point in Karen culture [is] if you turn eighteen, we don't want our children to get off [to] move out from the families. We stay living together and working, we maintain for inspiring the family life. This is a little bit different. We don't want the independent life for the family."

Josiah is in the Twin Cities with his wife, Daisy, and their three children. Josiah's oldest daughter studies biology at St. Olaf. His son is a senior in high school, and his younger daughter is in eighth grade. "My children still have a very tight connection with us, even when they are going to college," he says. "They don't keep far away; they are always connected with us."

"Let's talk about the Karen situation in Twin Cities," he continues. "We have a lot of Karen [who] came to the US and to join families in the Twin Cities, especially in St. Paul. So we build the community and we do work for the community's development. Now we have our own church, do you know that? The [first] Karens joined the American First Baptist church in downtown St. Paul, but the community split up. One stayed at the First American Baptist church, but my church moved out because the congregation was growing. We are more conservative, more like the Evangelical style, so now we have our own church. First Karen Baptist church in St. Paul has an Irish minister. We try to build up our families to grow spiritually and as well we are working to support our community."

Josiah has recently returned to school to study community ministry leadership. "We try to support sharing the responsibility among the community. We have the regular meeting every Sunday and every Saturday, so it's very exciting and pretty busy.

"I will be with [MCC] Refugee Services for a while, but this is kind of like the ministry to the people. People come from around the world, [and we are] helping them to be self-sufficient in the United States. I love to do that. [It's] so amazing. I am so blessed to know people [from] around the world, people from cross cultures. So I am still going on working unless they terminate me."[34]

Josiah laughs. "So," he says, "that is my life."

---

34. Josiah worked at MCC Refugee Services until December 2009 when he left to become the Refugee Community Liaison at the District 6 Planning Council in St. Paul. He has since left this position to focus on his pastoral ministry to the Karen community.

Zimbabwe

Zimbabwe gained independence from Great Britain in 1980, and Robert Mugabe became the new nation's first postcolonial ruler. During his tenure, his policies have crippled Zimbabwe's economy with runaway inflation and unemployment over 90 percent, and he has firmly opposed relinquishing political power. The international community has accused him of rigging elections.[35]

Over twenty-three thousand refugees have fled, most of them to camps in neighboring Botswana and South Africa.[36] As a result of the lack of economic opportunities, refugees from all ethnicities and social classes have fled President Mugabe's political persecution.[37]

English is Zimbabwe's official language, although many people speak tribal languages and dialects. The majority of the population practices Christianity, while indigenous beliefs and Islam are also prominent.

Zimbabwe is a landlocked country in south-central Africa, and it has a tropical climate with a rainy season that lasts from November to March. It shares a mountainous eastern border with Mozambique. Victoria Falls, the world's largest waterfall, is located on its northern border with Zambia.[38]

---

35. CIA World Factbook, "Zimbabwe."

36. UNHCR.org, "Zimbabwe."

37. CNN.com, "Thousands Flee into South Africa a Day."

38. CIA World Factbook, "Zimbabwe."

Malaba:
Former Prisoner, Family Man

"Goodnews Malaba" tells his story on a rainy September afternoon, a few weeks after starting computer classes at MCC Refugee Services. As usual, he's neatly dressed in slacks and a button-down shirt. His native language is Shona, but he speaks very articulately in British-accented English.

Malaba was born in Zimbabwe in the 1960s. "I grew up in a large family," he begins. "My father had more than two wives and had eighteen children. Immediately after marrying my mother, my father married another woman.

"It was a surprise [to my mother], but the girl was pregnant and had to be married. We don't encourage divorce. During that time, divorce was very difficult. She told him, 'It's up to you.' That's how he married these two, and then he got all his wives and went to the town where he was working. He got another job on another farm, in a different town, which was a little bit closer to our place along Harare to Mutare highway."

"The eastern part of Zimbabwe is a very beautiful land, with mountains. The highest mountain in Zimbabwe is called Nyangani Mountain and is in our area. I was born in Rusape and grew up there. We went to school, but girls did not go far. During that time, there was no enforcement of law to let girls go to school. Also, they thought that boys will grow up to be the head of the family; when women grow up, they will be married to a boy who is the head and has good work. That was the whole idea.

"I was very cautious in my life, and it happened that maybe my mother liked me a lot, and maybe I was a very obedient person. I did everything and also was smart—in school I did very well." Malaba was the only one out of his father's eighteen children to attend college. "So it happened that I was a little bit different. I was the youngest boy in the family, and because of that my father chanced to like me a lot.

"I was very much after my mother, having to learn everything. I learned cooking. That helped me because the elementary school was very far away, so I would take all my belongings and stay at the school for the week, cooking my own food.

"Then, if it is Saturday, the students would go home. I remember when I was very young, I was going home and I met people who believed in ritual sacrifice..." Here Malaba pauses as though thinking about how to explain.

"Not animal sacrifice." He hesitates and then speaks carefully. "They believe in killing people—but they don't sacrifice to God. It's for the *business*." His voice drops lower as he seeks to explain. "What I mean is, if you're a businessman, you go to a witch doctor. The witch doctor says, 'For your business to grow up, you need to do these certain things.'

"These business people send people into the bush to wait for the young ones. If they catch you, they kill you, and after killing they take all things like ears, nose, eyes...even your private parts! Then they dump you like that, even females. They give the body parts to the witch doctor, who mixes them with medicine. Bush medicine. He gives that to one who wants to make business. The witch doctor says, 'This is your medicine now, for your business to be lucrative. To be viable. To be outstanding. To make you a lot of money.' Of course it's illegal—if you are caught, it's just like any murder.

"I met two of these people, after they had hidden in the bush. Like I said, I come from mountainous country—there are even rivers to cross when going home. I was alone, because my brothers had grown up. I was maybe seven or eight. Very little.

"So I hear someone whistling, you know." He whistles softly. "It just astonished me. I was just perplexed, you know—*What is this?* I thought.

"He was calling someone who was ahead, saying in code that there is a young boy coming. When I heard that, I did not proceed along the way. I went into the bush. I was scared. I climbed into the hill, and by the time I looked back, I saw one of them looking for me. I had heard that there were people like this, because we heard all kinds of stories and warnings.

"Then one saw me on the hill! So he ran after me, and I ran away to the other side of the hill! But he was after me, running!" Malaba shakes his head. "I ran as fast as I could. I *ran*, but he was still after me. I ran until I saw a stranger—not one of these guys, but just another person who heard the noise as I was running and crying at the same time.

"When I saw him, I thought he was also one of the guys, one of the *people!*" Malaba laughs. "Oh my, I was so very afraid. I just ran again. But I noticed that he was not after me, and he said, 'No, no, no, look here—' and I said, 'No, no, the people who want to kill me, they are following me!'

"He knew about it, this guy. He said, 'Oh, yeah.' He knew. He waited for those people to see who they were. But they saw him and went away. This guy followed me until I was at home. I said to my mother, 'They wanted to kill me! And I saw this guy, and I thought, he is one of them!'" He laughs, shaking his head at the memory. "He explained himself and happened to be known by my parents for his innocence.

"There are such stories, you know. You could hear some stories that someone was found dead and decapitated and this is what happened. The killing, it was there, in the bushes. From there on I said, 'Oh, my God. I will never ever forget that episode, that day.' I was so young. To this day it is in my memories."

After completing high school, Malaba went to the capital of Zimbabwe, Harare, to stay with his brothers. Then he spent two years in the United Kingdom. "When I came back, I continued going to the university and thought about joining a financial institution.

"In Harare, that's where I met my wife. She was just completing her own college, and we just talked. We just connected as friends until we had a relationship deeper than a friendship. We decided to marry, and that was that."

He says that they didn't have what he calls a white wedding until later; at the time, they just signed the certificate. "*Labola*[39] was very good," Malaba remembers. "It was during good times, these days. I remember it was fifty thousand.[40] It was a lot of money, anyway, including cows—we normally pay cattle as well. And then money on top, that is what you call labola.

"I remember one day there was a debate. Some men were saying, 'You know, women are very disadvantaged—or girls, ladies—if they first love someone, there is nothing they can do in order to get him to oneself. You know, women cannot propose. If you do it, you are taking the other way around. So as a result women are sometimes married to someone you don't love!' Maybe it just happens that you come along somebody and he's better than nothing."

The story turns to talking about his career and the inflation in Zimbabwe. "When I joined the bank, things in Zimbabwe were very good. Banks were expanding, new banks were started. The economy was very good. One day, I remember, our money was even stronger than the British pound! It was 1980 or earlier. Things were stable, although problems were emerging bit by bit.

Then came 1997. "Now we have not enough maize for the country, for the people, and our staple food is maize.[41] And all those things were just gripping, right? The government, overlooking all those problems, went on. The government thought the war veterans might revolt, and they said, 'Okay, we want to give you gratitude. We want to give you money, because of what you did during the war; you are the ones who got us this independence.'

"So they printed money. They gave a lump sum of one hundred thousand to those people, war veterans, who would also get a certain amount

---

39. Bride price or bride wealth, similar to a dowry, except the groom pays it.

40. Fifty thousand Zimbabwean dollars (ZWD).

41. Corn, which dominates Zimbabwe's agricultural industry.

of money monthly, maybe five thousand or ten thousand. They were shrinking the economy, giving these people a lot of money. Companies were no longer efficient, goods were scarce. There's a lot of money, a lot of people to buy those goods, and therefore shortages of goods was created. Hence, that was not enough.

"The government went on to do something else, because they were going into election season, they thought of something to please the masses. How can they please the masses? They said all the white people were actually holding the economy in their hands by controlling land agriculture in farming and had to be chased away. The government said, 'You, a white person, you are not originally from Zimbabwe. You come from England, wherever and whatever, you have to go.' They created gangsters of those people they were giving some money before, the war vets and other ZANU PF[42] party-affiliated people, and they grabbed the white people's farms. Officially, the gangsters were war vets. But they were supported by the government.

"So these people, they could go to the farms, they could say, if you won't do this and do what they ask, they will chop your head, kill you, or even your family. You have to run. And you have to leave everything!" Malaba throws up his hands. "You don't even carry anything. So, go as you are! Leave your tractor outside, leave your car outside, and everything, go! Just go! If you don't and resist to go, they axed people alive and burned people alive, including babies, too. They were merciless killers, like deadly animals. You could hear of bloodshed for human beings happening in the farms all over the country.

"These people who are in the farming now, who grabbed the farms, they don't even have the know-how of farming. Who got the farms? Mugabe's people. Tobacco is a very essential commodity to grow and it needs a lot of money, inputs. No one could do that. Maize, no one could grow. Wheat, nothing. This was coupled with drought and distractions of irrigation infrastructure. No foreign currency. There is nothing to export.

---

42. ZANU PF, the governing political party.

Those people were hungry but they grabbed the farms and now they cannot do anything to feed themselves.

"And when they crippled the economy, they said the Western people are the people who have put sanctions on us. But they have forgotten their mismanagement of the economy. They have forgotten about the killings of the white people who had the know-how of farming. They have forgotten that they grabbed the mines. They have forgotten their corruption. They have forgotten all of that.

"I was working. The bank used to pay my fees; I had a commercial company car, and fuel was taken care of by the company. It was very comfortable. Myself, I was comfortable. But other people who were working in industry were not—many people were laid off because companies could not go any further, and no new companies formed.

"We speak of billions and trillions, quadrillions of dollars in Zimbabwe right now. People who thought of it right from the beginning ran away to other countries."

Malaba trails off and he leans in closer and pauses. "Now come to my world," he says, his voice soft. "I was working in a bank, in a financial institution. And I thought myself, 'No, this is too much.'

"By 2000, a new party had formed. They said, 'Now, look here. The direction things are going, that this country is going, will be worse.' They started a new party, which was led by Tsvangirai—the MDC.[43] This party was against Mugabe. So it happened that I joined this, in our area.

"That is when my story—my big story—comes from. I joined them, and I became one of their outstanding people. I was very well spoken of. You know, [I] was enticing people to join the new party against the government. That was what the government doesn't like.

"We knew that it was dangerous, because of things that happened before. But we had no choice. We had no choice here. And there are people who have died because of that. I just thought to myself, maybe things will be better off, since we are heading for election next year.

"Within the middle of this, they came to my workplace. I was not

---

43. The Movement for Democratic Change, led by Morgan Tsvangirai.

there. They searched for my house, and they came to the house where I was staying. One day I met them, and that's when they hit me here. You see this scar? That's where they hit me here. The ZANU PF militia, known as the 'green bombers,' wanted to kill me. I was unconscious—they thought I was dead.

"I was taken by neighbors and good Samaritans to the hospital, gained my consciousness. They thought I was dead, but I was not. After some time, they heard that I was still alive. So they searched for me again, but this time I escaped. They killed everything at home—my dogs—and hit my wife and everything…and then…" He trails off. "That's when I decided, now the best thing is to run away from this place before they kill me.

"My wife worked for the government. She was very smart; she did not want to involve herself in these politics. She said that, 'No, it's only my husband.' Although I knew that my wife doesn't support the government, but that's why she remained a little bit safe. She was safe.

"I just told my wife that 'I'm moving away, this is the case. But I don't know where I'm going to land, whether I'll come back or not. And don't tell the children; they will tell the government, otherwise there will be problems for them here.' It happened that my wife has a cousin who works in the Democratic Republic of the Congo. The cousin came to Zimbabwe, and I heard of her. I was not at home; I was in hiding. I went to her and she told me that she expected this. She asked, 'What is it that you can do now?' And I said, 'Run away.'

"Where? It happened that I had a visa for the United States from my travel with the bank. She funded me some money, and I bought a ticket. I came from South Africa to Washington. But in Washington, you have to go to my intended state on what is called a domestic flight. So in other words, you have to declare yourself at the border in Washington. That's when I declared myself.

"Because of telling the truth, because of that, they said, 'You must be detained.' Then I went to prison. I was in detention for about two months. When I was there, that's when lawyers and so forth worked things out for me. The federal government found out that I had never done anything criminal, and back at home there was no violation of any law either. They decided to grant me parole. And I was out.

"Whilst I was in detention, my lawyers found the address for a cousin in Minnesota. They phoned him, and he said, 'Oh, you can come,' and that's why I ended up here. I stayed with him for a while, but he is married, his family is also here, and he is not prepared for this.

"When I came to the United States, what happened in my country was always a fresh thing in my mind, and if I thought about that I could end up shedding tears. In other words, mentally, I was affected."

"These police are good, but when you are in prison, a prisoner, they are very ruthless. They are ruthless—I mean it. You know, they could tie me, they could put chain here." He motions to his wrists. "Put chain here." He motions to his ankles. "And tie here." He motions to his waist. "And put chains on my leg, as if I had killed someone. Oh, it was horrible. That's when I started having high blood pressure. It was horrible. It was so horrible. In my life I have never been in prison, and that is the first time I ever had any chains; that is my first time I ever lived in prison. Oh, boy, it was a very horrible: hard time for me, to be in prison."

He begins to talk about his life since being released and coming to Minnesota. "What I often discover here in the United States is that the culture is very different from our culture." He nods. "Here, if people don't know you, you are isolated. you will not have any friends at all. To make friends is very difficult—very, very difficult, I mean to say. And if you want help and people don't know you, you also have problems. They don't entertain strangers.

"Life here was very hard at first, because when I came it was during the cold season. I had to stay indoors. I thought to myself, if I could I would have gone back home! And if it wasn't for the problems I had there, I would have gone back!"

Malaba begins to explain recent politics in Zimbabwe.

"After all those elections, a lot of people have been killed. The person I am supporting won the first elections, and they did not want to announce that; they said that he won but not enough. Not the fifty percent. But honestly speaking, he won more than fifty percent. So they arranged for another election. And those war veteran people, soldiers, police, they went into villages everywhere, beating everyone who voted for the opposition, and lot of people, more than two hundred, have been killed.

"And what happened? Tsvangirai saw that this is exactly what is happening, and he pulled out. Mugabe said okay: he declared himself a winner. And now? Everybody was crying, and he cannot do anything to the economy right now—it is plunging and plunging deeper, until everyone, even his supporters, have *felt* it now, that this is too bad.

"So they had to have some talks. I have heard that they are now agreed to share the power. I haven't seen the outline of the power sharing, but I understand that if they can do that to the benefit of the people in Zimbabwe, and if Tsvangirai has more power, maybe things will start going better. They might stop the killings completely. Especially if Tsvangirai controls the police and the army.

"That's the situation up to now. They have joined together, but I'm not sure about them. I don't trust them anymore. Because when you know the leadership the way I know this Mugabe's leadership...there is something, somewhere, wrong right now. People are still in camps. They are still beating people. There is violence. And at the same time, I have heard that the people who were arrested in the opposition party are still in prison. Quite a lot of them, fifteen thousand, maybe ten thousand are still in prison."

Malaba says that ideally, instead of trying to return to Zimbabwe, he will bring his family to the United States. "The Advocates[44] are starting the application to bring my family here. Because I cannot stay here alone forever. If that happens, it means I have to marry again here! Because if they cannot come, and I cannot go, what can you do? You can't be alone for a long, long time, especially when you were once married. Because they're different, single life and married life—they are completely different. I don't even remember when I last had a single life. Which I

---

44. The Advocates for Human Rights, a nonprofit based at the University of Minnesota.

understand you shouldn't have for a long time, you know, the single life; otherwise, you forget about all the marriedness. It's just not good. In an ideal world, I think my family should come here. But the only thing I can do right now is just to start over. Just to start over, and forget about a lot of things."

Seven months after this interview, Malaba started a job as a cleaner for an apartment building. Later, he left that job and trained in the financial sector for six months. Because of the slow economy, Malaba is still searching for a job and hoping the job market will improve. He continues to wait for the day that his wife and five children can join him in the United States.

Maka:

Motivated Mother, Determined Advocate

Maka comes to the office to tell her story. She arrives a half an hour late because of the snow that is blowing havoc across the roads—and the bus she took from St. Paul was extra slow. She wears a thick winter coat that she removes as she sits down in the soft chair in MCC's "living room" space. She is a sturdy woman who walks and speaks with authority. She winds her long hair in small, loose braids; it is dark brown with blonde extensions added in, and is tied back in a thick ponytail. It is impossible to deduce from her appearance that she is an asylee living in a homeless shelter. Maka tells her story carefully, but with conviction. She is still in the heat of struggle and her deep voice tells her story with weariness and passion.

"I was born in Harare. It was called Sallsbury when we were under the British colony at that time. I was born at Harare hospital. I have lived the rest of my life in Zimbabwe. I did my primary education, my secondary education. I've been to university in Zimbabwe. I was working for the past twenty years in Zimbabwe. I got married in Zimbabwe. I have two kids, seventeen and fifteen. I had a home in Zimbabwe. That was my life." Maka folds her hands on her lap, pausing as she considers her history.

"I worked as a legal secretary for nine years, and then I worked as an administrator for twelve years. Am I right? Yes, a patient administrator. At a local company in Zimbabwe. My husband was an accountant for one of the insurance companies in Zimbabwe. By the time he left, he was the chief accountant at that company."

Maka and her husband lived in Mount Pleasant, a town near the big capital city of Harare where she grew up. Her parents were teachers in Harare, she says.

"As I grew up, I knew there was war going on, but it was mostly in the rural areas. But in Harare, I never came across anything. I was twelve when we got our independence. Until then, it was so peaceful. Until 2008, that's when things started affecting my life. Otherwise, all along, it was peaceful. They were different this year, but I was a nonpartisan. I wasn't involved in politics. I had my job. I would contribute when discussing with other people, but I was not active in politics. Except for my husband was the one who was kind of active in politics, but without my knowledge, because I wasn't approving of it."

Maka launches into the explanation of how life fell apart for her family.

"In 2008, we were going to have elections to change the government. I knew my husband wanted—was involved—but I didn't know he was directly involved. Because he knew I wasn't for the idea, because of the dangers involved in being in politics. So he took leave: he went on leave, on vacation, and he told me he was doing some study outside the town, but I didn't know he was campaigning for the opposition party. It was his rural home, it was where the president of Zimbabwe, Mugabe, comes from. It was the president's constituency. It was a very volatile constituency.

"I don't know what gave him the guts to do such a thing. Anyways, so this is where all the problems started. Because they were after him. They wanted him. And he went into hiding immediately after we were attacked the first time. And when I called the opposition party, they had to take him into hiding immediately. And we thought it was over, because they came home looking for him. And they didn't find him. Initially we thought he was dead. We only learned he was alive about three months ago. So that's how things began. He was missing for three years, five months now. We haven't been together, but he was found in the UK now. Yeah, they took him from Zimbabwe to Malawi, from Malawi to Sierra

Leone, from Sierra Leone to the UK. He had no passport, so he is in the UK right now. I just got to know about it three months ago."

Maka explains that when she found out her husband was alive, she had very mixed feelings.

"After what I went through, I didn't have any excitement. Anyway, I was happy to know that he was alive, but I can't say my feelings. I don't know what to feel. I don't know what to think. Yeah. I've been through a lot. I've been through a lot, because of his decision to be involved in politics. Yeah, yeah. Myself and the kids have been through a lot. So, well, part of me blames him. Part of me says, 'Okay, who else could have done it? If he wouldn't do it?'" She sighs, looking sad. "So, that's how I feel about it."

When her husband disappeared Maka's life initially continued like normal. "I was still working. I was still living my life. My kids were still going to school. Life was normal. Then we had the first attack. The first time, they didn't beat us or anything. They just locked us in a room and they just turned the house upside down. They were looking for—whatever they were looking for, they didn't find it. We thought that was the end of it. They weren't going to come back for me or for anything else."

Maka explains that the people who came worked for the new ruling government.

"That was the first time. And then they came back, when they didn't find him, they went to his parent's home. In the rural area. And they didn't find him. They burned the houses, three houses. Up to now I don't know where my in-laws are, because they had to run for their lives. I don't know where they went into hiding; I don't know where they are now. I don't have any way to find out where they are! Yeah. So when they couldn't find him, they were quiet for a bit of some time. And we had elections. When the opposition party won, and if you were watching what happened, if you were following the elections of Zimbabwe. Then they started again. They started again. That's when I had a very nasty experience—yeah—which prompted me to leave the country until today.

"They beat me up and I went into hospital. I was unconscious. These are some of the marks." Maka pauses to point to a quarter inch long indentation on her dark brown skin, about two inches below her right eye. "And, uh, I went into hiding with the kids."

Maka's voice becomes slower, and she sounds tired as she tells the story.

"We went to Masvingo. We lived there for almost three, four months. And then when they started calling for meetings—to attend the ruling party meetings—and I was not going to those meetings. The neighbor people saw me, I think. And she reported me. And then my friend had to ask me to go to Botswana. And the lady who I was supposed to find in Botswana was not there. She had just moved. So I lived in—what do you call it? A lodge, for about one week. And I didn't have enough money. And I was running out of money and I had children. So I had to go back to Masvingo. When I got back to Masvingo, my friend had been beaten. They were accusing her of keeping sellouts from Harare.

"So I couldn't stay there with the kids. I had to leave. She had to call another friend of hers in Mutare, so I went to Mutare. I left the kids in Mutare and went to South Africa, tried to seek asylum in South Africa. But that was the time these xenophobic attacks were serious. They were killing Zimbabweans; they were beating up Zimbabweans, saying 'Go back to your country. You are taking our jobs. Go back to Zimbabwe.' So I had to go back, back to Zimbabwe. And I stayed in Mutare in some time, and then that's when the government was announcing that it was going to be the government of national unity. That there is going to be reconciliation. The impression was so encouraging, to the point that I was convinced that things are changing. Things are getting back to the normal state of life. So I decided, three months later, to go back home. So I went back home to my kids.

"I went back home and I stayed home, until this day I decided to go and pay my electricity bills in town, so I was driving. As I was driving, I saw a car with dark-tinted windows following me. And—" Maka pauses before continuing with calm and measured words, "I knew, I knew this car was not going anywhere. It was trying to follow me. Because the security of the opposition party, they had come, when I went back home, and tried to help me, security wise, to coach me and train me to watch out for cars, especially cars like this. Because they used dark-tinted glass, because you can't see the people inside. I tried to change the direction of where I was going. I tried to change it for the third time, and I knew that these people were definitely following me.

"So what I decided to do was go straight into town. Because the other time I had seen a car following me before this one, and I went into the police station, they had refused to take my statement. And knowing that the police will never support you when you are saying you are from the other party, or your kids are related to the other party, they will never assist you. So what I decided to do was go and park right in the middle of the town, where there were public people.

"When I did that, I don't know how fast it was, I didn't see where they parked. But when I came out, immediately after I left my car I saw a man there, and another man there. And they were putting something here." She presses her hand into her right side. "I don't know what it was. One of the guys slapped me and said, 'Where is your husband?' And then, I—instead of answering, I screamed!" Her voice abruptly becomes loud. "And when I screamed, they saw that people just stopped. And there were so many people around. It was in the street. The two men let go of me and they said, 'Oh, we are going to come back for you. It's either your head or your husband.'

"You know, that's how bad it was, the last time I had to leave the country. I couldn't drive, they just pushed me, and then they left. And then these people came and asked me, 'What's wrong? What happened?' I explained that I couldn't drive. I was shivering. So one of these couple, they said, 'Okay, we'll drive you to the MDC office.' They drove me to the opposition party's office. When we got there, and they explained, they knew me now; they knew everything. They said, 'You know what? You just have to leave the country. You need to leave now. Not even tomorrow. You just need to leave now.'

"And I had to go back home, get the kids immediately. They gave me a driver. We got home, I took the kids immediately. It was just like picking up whatever I could at that time. And we left for Mutare, because when we were there, when I was packing, a phone rang. I picked it up.

And they said, 'You know what? Either your head, or your husband. You are going to die. Either you produce your husband or we want your head.' And you know, having gone through what I had already gone through, I knew they meant it.

"So I just had to leave that very same afternoon. And we got to Mutare. When we got to Mutare, they had got to that woman's house, because they knew we had been living there. I don't know how they got to know about it. But she had been beaten, and they had threatened to kill her and the family." Maka stops speaking for a moment.

"So we couldn't live there. So this guy had to call immediately the opposition party's office. And they said, 'You have to leave the country in that situation.' I said, 'Where can I go? I can't go to South Africa. What can I do?' They said, 'Don't you have any other place?' So I checked my passport—I still had a USA visa, because I meant to come to the US another time with my husband for a holiday. So I still had that visa in my passport. So I said, 'Okay, I have a US visa.' But I didn't know anybody. So they said, 'Okay, go.' And they bought the ticket immediately.

"And I just had to leave that very same day. On my way I met this old woman who I don't really know. I don't know anything about her. I just asked her to take my kids, or find somebody else to take my kids." She pauses again. "So that's how I left Zimbabwe.

"I didn't know anybody. I didn't have any family. And the ticket I had was for JFK in New York. I didn't know where to go. I didn't have enough money. I had about three hundred dollars, two hundred fifty I think. That's all I had. So it was very difficult for me."

Maka says she arrived in New York in December 2009 on a visitor's visa.

"So when I was getting my luggage, after I got my luggage, I was going to ask where I could seek asylum. So when I saw a policeman and asked him, he just said, 'You can go and seek asylum in the airport, but if you seek asylum in the airport, they will lock you up. But if you know anybody, go into America and seek asylum from within. Because if you seek it here, they are going to lock you up, lock you up in prison.'

"So I had no choice. I had to go out. And one of these guys, he had a laptop. So I asked, 'Can I check on Facebook. Maybe I can come across anyone from Africa, from Zimbabwe, or something like that.' And just fortunately, I found somebody with a name and a phone number. For some reason on Facebook, you never get phone numbers. But here was a phone number. So I called it; I explained my story. She said she lived in Minnesota, but she was going to be leaving within three weeks. So she would welcome me, and then I would find out what else to do once she leaves.

"So I came here by Greyhound bus. She took care of me for about three weeks. And then she was moving. So I started living with different people from one place to another. You know, in the church…she had introduced me to a Methodist church. And people there, they knew my story, so they were taking me in for like a week, and then another week. And then somebody else would take me in for a week. Until I found the shelter I am living right now, currently. So that's how I came here."

Maka came to Minnesota in the dead of winter, when the temperature difference is the severest from the warm climate in Zimbabwe.

"It was terrible. Because in my country, it was raining, but it was very hot. And I didn't have warm clothes, I didn't have blankets. I really didn't have anything warm. But this woman was so good. She bought me a jacket. She bought me warm clothes. She tried her best, she did."

Maka explains that she applied for asylum soon after arriving, a process that can take months, and even years, to complete.

"For me it was very long, given the scenario and the situation I was in. And the situation my family is in right now. To me it was very long; it was very, very long. Because I came here in December, I filed in December. I only got an interview in April. But they were saying it was very fast according to other people. They were telling me they waited two years to get an interview. But for me, given my situation, it wasn't fast enough!

"So I had my interview on the 30th of April. I got my asylum on the second of June. And, um, I started applying—that was the most painful thing for me—to start applying for my family, for my children and my husband. Which only got approved when I approached Senator Klobuchar right now. Because I was so desperate. I don't know the safety of my children. I don't know where they are. Everything surrounding the situation is just so hard. So I just got my children's petition approved. And right now, the people, the women with whom I live, they are trying to raise money for my children's air tickets. Because I have tried every agent to seek help. I have tried the senator, to ask her if she could try and get, help me find, either a loan to bring my children. She couldn't find it.

"I was desperate. So the women who I know from the church and some other women, they are the ones who are raising bit by bit, asking people to donate their mileage. Some are donating cash. So far for the people in Botswana who are going into Zimbabwe to look for my children. We have raised seven hundred dollars for the people to go into Zimbabwe and look for the children. *But*, I have my children's passports with me. I asked the immigration if they could just put the visas on the passports, my children's passports. Or if they could. I couldn't send it by DHL to Zimbabwe, because I knew that it wouldn't get there. Or I was asking them, when they send my file to Africa, if they could put the passports in the file for safe transmission. Nothing worked out. So I have a challenge right now. Whether to go to Africa, I don't have the effort to. If I send them by DHL, I don't know if they are going to get there. So I am caught between—if they find the kids, how are they going to bring them into Botswana? And there is going to be another process for them to get their visas for them to come here too, and the buying of their air tickets. And right now I am in the middle of looking for an apartment. I don't have any accommodations.

Maka has not heard from her children since she left them with the old woman in Botswana before she came to the United States a year ago. She says it has been a challenge, but she has found support here in Minnesota.

"The people from the Center for Victims of Torture (CVT) have been very helpful. I went through the program of the groups, of counseling. They have really been helpful. Also people from the church, you know, they've also been so, so helpful. They just keep encouraging you. You know it's not easy. Sometimes it is very difficult to understand what is happening to you. Another day you are there, another day you are here…you are never predictable. You are never yourself. That's all I can tell you. You are never yourself when you are in the situation I am in right now. It's kind of a real challenge.

"In Africa, the impression that we get from the media is that once you get to UK or America, to these Western countries, you just think you will be safe and they will help you be safe with your family. You know, that's the only thing that will be on your mind. And you get here." She says loudly, "It's so hard to be able—to be safe is so hard, you don't have this asylum to start with. They don't care about you. They will have nothing to do with you. You live in the shelter. You have no home." Maka still speaks adamantly, but there is sadness there now. "You get the asylum. Before then, you can't be working. You get the asylum, you can't still get your family, they have programs running—it's okay, but really, you know, given the needs and the agents in this situation, it's so hard and sometimes you find that the resources they are not user friendly.

"So, it's very hard. Especially for asylees. Maybe refugees are better, but for asylees[45], really I have seen that it is so, so hard to the point that I am looking for women who would like to advocate for asylees. I am really prepared to work with women who really want to—because what I have gone through.

"You know, if we look at this democracy, this is not democracy! If we are thinking of human rights—they are being violated. I would be so happy to have, you know, women groups who are really willing to stand up and, you know, speak out on what asylees go through. Because I don't get it why there should be a difference between a refugee and asylee. It's not fair! I don't get it!" Maka is clearly frustrated. "Because for a refugee, your family is in camps, right? They can be able to bring their family with the help of their agents. They can actually loan money or give money. So they bring their families into safety. But for asylees, there is nothing like that. Which is the most important part is safety! Even if I live in a shelter

---

45. Refugees and asylees both meet the same conditions of persecution and inability to return to their homeland. The only significant difference is in where the status was granted. Refugees receive their status overseas, before coming to the US. Asylees first make their way to the US, usually by means of a valid visa, and apply for asylum in the US. Once asylum status is granted, refugees and asylees are treated the same as refugees in regard to public benefits and immigration status, except that asylees do not receive initial resettlement assistance.

with my family, but knowing that I am safe, I can work through things. It's okay.

"All these other resources are okay, but they are not very important right now where I am concerned. Because right now what I am concerned with is the safety of my children and my husband. I don't know where they are! That's the big issue right now.

"How can I be so comfortable when I don't know where my kids are? How can I be comfortable when I don't know what my children are eating? How can I be comfortable when I don't know whether they are still alive or dead? How can you expect me to go get the food stamps and eat comfortably? For your information, I can't even eat. I can't sleep!" Maka pauses to catch her breath. "I don't even have the strong will to do anything! Because your mind is so...you know." She sighs heavily. "Sorry, but...it's just...a lot. How to explain this? I don't expect them to understand it, because they've never been there. I don't expect them to understand it. I really don't. Yeah." Maka pauses again. "Because they've never walked that road. If when they look at you they want to give you drugs, try and give you some medication thinking you are crazy. No, I am not crazy. But I am in a situation that needs to be addressed immediately. Yeah. I'm not crazy." Maka stops speaking now, taking long, deep breaths.

"I'm just hoping the United Nations or the Red Cross will find the children. That's my biggest hope. And once they find them, I am hoping I might probably find assistance for their air tickets. Yeah, because currently I am not working. I don't have a job. I don't have a home. You know, it has been like a roller coaster trying to get a home. They say find an apartment, but the kind of restrictions that they have for you is like really suffocating! They tell you that you are here alone. You have to get a studio, get a six-month contract and within those six months, if you receive your family, the studio, they are not prepared to live with you there. You can't bring your family in that studio. And on the other hand, you've got a lease. So if you want to move you have to pay—I mean, can't you see this is really weird? It's really weird," she says with incredulity. "I had this lease for six months. I'm expecting my family to be coming. That will be four people in the studio. And the owner of the studio can't take me in with four people! And I don't have anywhere to put my children if they come now. I don't have anywhere to take them to. I don't have family here. The shelter that I am living is Sisters of St. Joseph, they only take women! And they can't accommodate my family there. So...you know, it's just kind of like a roller coaster, you know. They say we are helping you, but there is always a catch. It's quite, you know, like, very difficult. Yeah. It's kind of really hard. I don't know, but that's the situation." Her voice has dropped almost to a whisper now.

"I just think the most important thing is the issue of safety. Yeah. You know, I think they really have to revise their laws, because it's not fair that you file for asylum, you file for your family. Because when I started filing in December, I put everything, including my family. Why should I apply again for my family? When it is the exact same thing I gave them the first time is the same thing I will put the second time! And we are talking about time and people's lives that are in danger! So where is the conscience about safety here? Where is it?

"Where is it? So...you know, I just—I understand, okay, they are doing it by the book, but I think it is too much paperwork at the expense of people's lives! If the USA claims to be what they really say they are, then they have to show to the world what they really are.

"I know you can never find fairness on earth, and democracy we are talking about, it's something that can never be followed. It can never be there. So, I might be wasting my breath. But anyway, that is the facts!" Maka finishes with a big sigh.

"It's good that we can talk about these things, because you know, when I couldn't talk about it. Going through counseling with this CVT has been helpful. I am able to talk about it. Like, okay, I am still in need, but at least I can say it out loud. I can say something that I was not able to all along. All I could do was just tears. I would just cry. But now? I appreciate all those people who have helped me to tell my story."

Shortly after telling her story, Maka heard news of her children and continues her efforts to bring them to the United States.

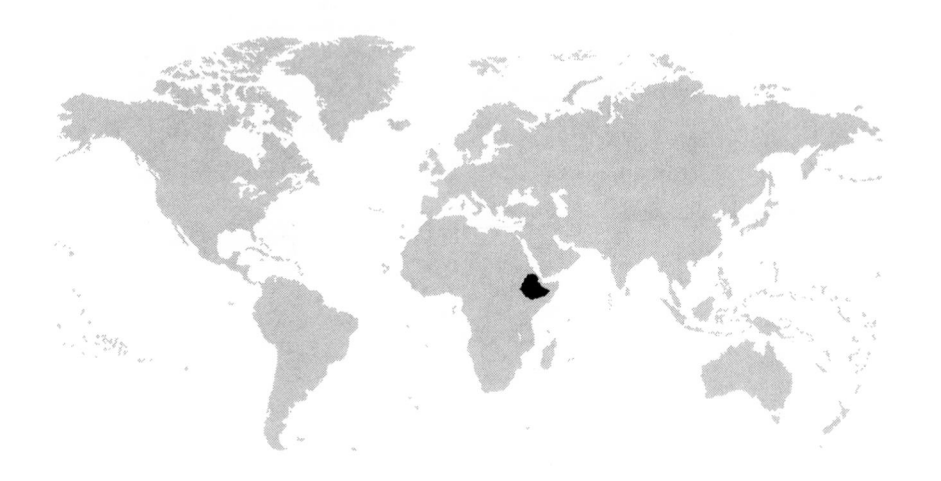

Ethiopia

Of more than one hundred ten thousand refugees originating from Ethiopia,[46] over five thousand have resettled in Minnesota since 1982.[47] Ethiopia is a landlocked country in East Africa, and has both sent refugees to its neighboring countries and received refugees from its neighbors, most frequently Eritrea and Somalia.

Ethiopia had not been colonized, but Emperor Haile Selassie ruled for much of the twentieth century. However, in 1973, his government was overthrown in a military coup.[48] The years following the coup saw civil wars amongst Ethiopia's ethnic groups, which led to Eritrea breaking away and forming its own country. Further, border disputes with Somalia increased unrest for civilians living in southeast Ethiopia. Complicating these conflicts were a series of severe droughts and famines in the 1980s and 1990s, as well as the spread of diseases due to poor sanitation and nutrition.[49]

The Ethiopian Highlands, a series of mountains, run from northwest to southeast, and the country has a tropical monsoon climate. Christianity

---

46. UNHCR.org, "Ethiopia."

47. MN Department of Health, "Primary Refugee Arrivals to Minnesota."

48. Baylor University, "Ethiopian Refugees."

49. Library of Congress website, "Refugees, Drought and Famine."

and Islam are the two largest religions in Ethiopia, and Amharic is the official language of the country. The Oromo, Ethiopia's largest ethnic group, speak Oromigna, and Tigrigna, the official language of present-day Eritrea, is also widely spoken.[50]

---

50. CIA World Factbook, "Ethiopia."

Hiruy:
Rights Holder, Seeker of Hope

One evening in late August, Hiruy tells his story from the comfort of his home on a tree-lined street in St. Paul. The curtains are drawn and the television in the corner is on mute, flickering uneven light across the room. In the kitchen, Hiruy's wife is cooking. Hiruy Gamada is an Oromo refugee who came from Ethiopia over five years ago.

"*Hiruy* means happiness, or something good. That is why my parents choose this name. And *Gamada* means to be happy. You know, in our country, when you name your daughter, your son, or someone like that, it has to have a meaning. We never name without meaning."

"I left my country because of the politics, so God knows. [My daughter] is born after I left my country, and came to Kenya. Her mother says, 'We will meet together when? God knows.' So she named her 'God Knows.'"

"[My parents were] simply farming there, you know, living a simple life." He had one sister and three brothers. "But except for one, they are not alive. They are older. One is younger. I don't know where he is now. Listen, we don't have any written history. We go and we start to live, and it…" He waves a hand. Then he says, "I came to Kenya around 1993. And I stayed there for nine years. I came to America in 2003 March. Now I'm here. I was born in 1948, so if you calculate…" He trails off.

He left Ethiopia because of the government. "This government is tribal. I was in prison for some days. Then, just after I escape from that, then I go to Kenya.

"When I say something, you have to understand," he says. "They are *tribal*. A tribal government. They chase other tribes, they think that everybody is against them. What can I say? It's not a democratic government. Since I came out of that country, politically, I can't go back."

He says it is difficult keeping in touch with family still in Ethiopia. "That's the problem. Just only by telephone and sometimes I am supporting them, when I am able to support them. But I myself do not go to Ethiopia while this government is in power."

After leaving his country, Hiruy was in a Kenyan refugee camp, and he describes what it was like for him. "Struggling. Sometimes working for somebody, but sometimes there was no money. Some people helped, but it was not a good life. I cannot tell you—I am living now in such a comfortable life. That was not a comfortable life."

After coming to Minnesota, he started to work. "I was working at a gas station for about four months. Then I was working at the airport. Then on top of that, I found a job in the University of Minnesota. I hope I am going to learn, too, you know, just working at the University of Minnesota," he adds, saying that he works in grounds and housekeeping management at the university. His wife works the same job.

Then the discussion moves on to his high-school-aged daughter. "She knows how to read and write [in Oromo], how to cook the food. She knows everything. She can choose whatever she likes, but we insist that she not forget our culture." Hiruy says he does not mind that she is growing up in a different culture, except perhaps for the competitiveness of the school system.

It's Sunday, and the talk naturally moves to religion. "We are not extremist," Hiruy says. "We are not dogmatic. We are believing. We accept one God. Everybody has the right to accept their own meaning, what is good, and to condemn others for their beliefs is not what I believe."

Hiruy says he recently became a citizen and though he says didn't study much, he passed the test.

"The policy of the United States is very nice. Just living their life, that is America," he answers. "Every guy has rights. For example, I bought this house. It's my house. It's my house! I am here for five years and now

I come to buy this. That's freedom. My own land, my own freedom—it's an exceptional right.

"Think about living in America. Rights are not for ethnicity. It's for all people living in America, and it's very nice. What can I say? This is a very good country. The constitution is very nice; you have good freedom. Politically, [you do not have] to be a Democrat or Republican, you have both: you have a choice. Such a nice thing. This is America. This is where I find myself.

"Nothing I miss [about Ethiopia], except…" He leans further back into the couch cushions. "I was born there. And the social life of that country and this country is different. But if you want, you can make a social life in this country also.

"Now we are living! We can make this, our traditional food. It is the same as if we are in Ethiopia. But now, this is my country! A guy says, 'Everybody, where he is, that is his country.' America is my country, Ethiopia is my country—where I am living, am working, that is my home. I have many privileges. We have a good, nice privilege. My daughter is going to school. And I don't miss anything, no. I can get my family by telephone or letters, or somewhat like that."

Hiruy doesn't seem to mind the Minnesota winters. "The weather? You can protect yourself according to the weather. When it is summer, wear summer clothes, in winter, those clothes." But he might not stay here for forever. "Let us say, change is the spice of life," he says.

He starts talking about the future. "I want to join this kind of [non-profit] organization. To try to help poor people. For example, in our country there are poor people that nobody will see. If they are helped, then tomorrow they improve themselves, they can live, working or doing something. When I was in Kenya, I couldn't help myself, and now I can. I will try to help people, to bring those poor people here.

"That is my first choice, to help others—not only from here, but from Africa, from wherever they are. This is my first ambition. I was helped by somebody, okay? And now I just have to also help somebody who is poor or has no means of getting this chance. Because of their lack of help, everything is closed to them. I hope it will happen. I will try, after I retire."

The clock on the wall chimes once more, and Hiruy shares one more thing. "The main, important thing is my vision. If it is possible—this is everybody's wish—but my wish is to secure this country. I don't know the way, but my dream is to go to school and learn something about security. First you secure yourself, then your home, then family, then your surroundings, then your town, your district, your state. [Until] everyone is secured. I want to gain some knowledge of this kind. Not easy to get. But that is another hope.

"Okay," Hiruy says with a note of finality in his voice. "That much I can tell you."

Munira:
Young Woman, Freedom Chaser

Munira, a young Oromo woman from Ethiopia, tells her story in the MCC office's "living room." She is known among the MCC staff as a strong-willed woman who speaks her mind—she is not afraid to tell you exactly what she thinks. She tells her story willingly, but with some apprehension. She has enough English to communicate effectively, but often struggles to find the words she wants to describe certain aspects of her story. With the language challenges comes a limitation in how much she shares—but what she does share gives a glimpse into the brave life of a young Muslim woman.

"I was born Dadar, Ethiopia...the small town. In the countryside. I have brother—one brother and six sisters. Including me. Yeah, we used to live together and after some time when I was ten or...fifteen...some night, some guys come to our neighbors. Some guys kill two guys in front of our door. And then, they catch my father and they took him and even my mother, they beat and take her. She take six months in jail. After that, we disappeared to come in Kenya. We lived in Kenya for eleven years."

Munira says that before she fled to Kenya she went to school until "class five." And her parents had their own business.

"They sell coffee—they have a coffee place, big store. And they have a car, they have big house. My father is a rich man. Yeah. After that we come Kenya. Even my sibling—two, three sibling—we left three sibling in Ethiopia. They are small; they are little. We left them with my grandmother."

They couldn't go back to Ethiopia for her younger siblings or to visit her grandmother.

"She is died. We hear, she is died. Even our siblings, we don't know where they living now, with whom they live—we don't have any idea. Even when we are coming to US, we lose our sister and my mother, all. They just disappeared. And then when we finish the process to come US, we find our mother. She come back, and finally we see each other when we come here. Now we call her, and we contact."

When they fled to Kenya on foot they did not go to a refugee camp.

"We are living in Nairobi. When our mother is there, we sell a coffee to someone. They have big mall, Somali mall... We sell tea or coffee there. After that when we lose our mother, we start to sell, to work hotel. Yeah, hotel restaurant."

Munira and her siblings lived together. "We lived with some ladies. After that, we disappeared. Some guys wanted to rape us. When Kenyans, they see you are a lady living alone, they want to use you. Some guys, he want to—to rape us, and he want to kill us. We were hiding someplace, me and my sister. And we live with our friend until we are coming to the US. We are living in hiding. Yeah, we didn't go straight like this one," Munira says, lightly touching her black head covering. "We cover our face. We didn't go without covering our face. We are afraid. Shocking— when we are going someplace, he found and followed us." They didn't know who this man was that was following them. "No, we don't know! He's foreigner. In Kenya, they live with foreigners...yeah, they live many cultures mixing. And...we are shocked! When we are coming to US, we come to be free now."

During this time in Kenya, Munira and her sister were not with their father; they had not seen him since 1996 when the first attack happened back in Ethiopia. "If he died? He's alive? We don't know about him."

"The men were coming," Munira says, pausing to clear her throat. "We don't know. We hear some guns. 'What happened?' we say. 'It's coming, Tigre's military.[51] A lot of them!' They came inside our home; they search it. Some guys are outside...some guy took this house. 'You have a gun?' they said. They took my father to beat him, and even my mom.

---

51. The military group ruling Ethiopia's government.

When they took my mom and my father, they take both of them separate! My mother they took to the police station, my father, we don't know where they put.

"They thought our family was coming to kill them. But we don't know who killed them; we don't know what happen to them...that time, we are kids. I think I am ten years? When I am living Kenya, I am fifteen. [At] that time, I am ten. Really, it was scary.

"Sometimes so bad! If you didn't...survive to live your life. You don't have freedom; when you go outside, the police catch you; they ask you for money. If you show 'I'm living legal,' you show a mandate, they cut your mandate; they don't care. Even the police in Kenya are thieves—many thieves, burglar. If you go straight on night, they beat you...even my sister, they want to rape her. One time my mom, me, and my sister, we are walking on the road, they catch my sister. Even I run. My mother—they— she lose her teeth, two teeth. After that, I cry loudly! Some guys coming and they...run away. And we go home. If we report to the police that thing, another day they come for us. We keep quiet. If we report it, then that guys coming next time. They know where we are living; they know about us. We are afraid, so we didn't say anything.

"Yeah, my brother and sister, they are living with us. Even my brother, he is...angry. Something he saw. We are lady; when we go straight, some guy want to beat us; he want to married us by forcing marriage—forcing marriage, he don't want this thing." Her brother was so angry by what was happening that he disappeared, she says.

On March 7, 2000, when they first arrived in Kenya, Munira and her family went to the United Nations offices where they received a mandate for ten years.

"We have mandate. When the UN give you mandate, you are have to go some place, safety place, to live your life in freedom, like to the US or other countries. When you take a mandate, it is necessary to go that place. You have your cases so dangerous after you.

"We told them, 'We are lady. We can't survive in this country. Some guys are running after us to rape us. When ladies are living alone; many guys, they abuse us.' After we told them, they accepted us for resettlement.

"When the flight is ready, we sign IOM. When we go to sign IOM, they told us to go to Minnesota. Before that, we didn't know where we are going. Yeah. They didn't mention it."

Munira and her sister were the first to get permission to come to the United States, and they came to Minnesota without knowing anybody else in the state. Munira was told, along with other refugees in a predeparture cultural orientation, some things about what to expect in the United States.

"They tell us the United States persons is nice, humble—when you go US, you go freedom, you work yourself. If you want to go school, you have—everything! It depends on you." But things were more difficult than she expected when she arrived in Minnesota. "This country, you must to have a car. You must have a job. We didn't find easily a job. Yeah, something is difficult."

Munira explains that she and her sister are waiting to bring their mother and other siblings to Minnesota to join them, with the help of a complicated immigration process.

Munira says that when she first arrived in Minnesota, it was the middle of July. "Oh, wow; when we are coming in summer...it's nice! Everything...we are feeling happy. Yeah..." MCC staff and her church cosponsorship group met Munira and her sister at the airport and brought them to their apartment.

"It's like...the apartment is not bad. For us, it's okay. We are new arrival. Yeah. But for now? We almost to finish our bill. They said eight months to help us, almost we finish. Must to get a job now. Yeah."[52] Munira has applied for lots of jobs, and she is hoping to get a housekeeping position soon. She and her sister are very worried about paying for rent in the coming months.

Munira says there are few things she misses about Ethiopia. "My family!" Her voice softens. "Ohhh...especially my family. No, no; nothing

---

52. When refugees are resettled in the US they receive a small, one-time transitional grant from the US government. Although refugees may qualify to receive public benefits, most often cash benefits are smaller than rental and other living expenses. Single adults receive 250 dollars per month for up to eight months through Refugee Cash Assistance.

else. Everything is here," Munira says emphatically. "They bring in here. If you want to buy something—culture, food, anything—it's here.

"My dream is to learn to be somebody, to stand to my life. To get what I want."

She wants people in Minnesota to know that the life of a refugee is not easy. Munira explains, "Refugees, when they live in camp or Nairobi, so difficult to live because—you know?—you are afraid of police, or something. You want even to eat; you didn't get enough to live. Even you—if you rent this house to get, if you don't have to pay money, thirteen day they throw you out, threw out, if you don't have money. A lot of people they go, like, crazy in Kenya. They think a lot of things. They don't get money, they don't get enough food—yeah. They can't survive their life. After that, they think," Munira says insistently, "night or day, they become crazy. So you don't have a future.

"If they go UN, ask them, if they didn't give them solution one time. Even if you want to go UN, you must have transport money. If you don't have money, you don't go. You stay home. If even you don't have a chance to get a mandate, to get a process."

Now that she is in Minnesota, Munira is happy. "Minnesota everything is good. I like it. The people, all the things—good. Only the weather, a little bit." Munira doesn't seem to mind the snow as much as some new arrivals do, but it is a big change from Ethiopia and Kenya.

"I wish all of my family, my mother, my sister, is coming to the US."

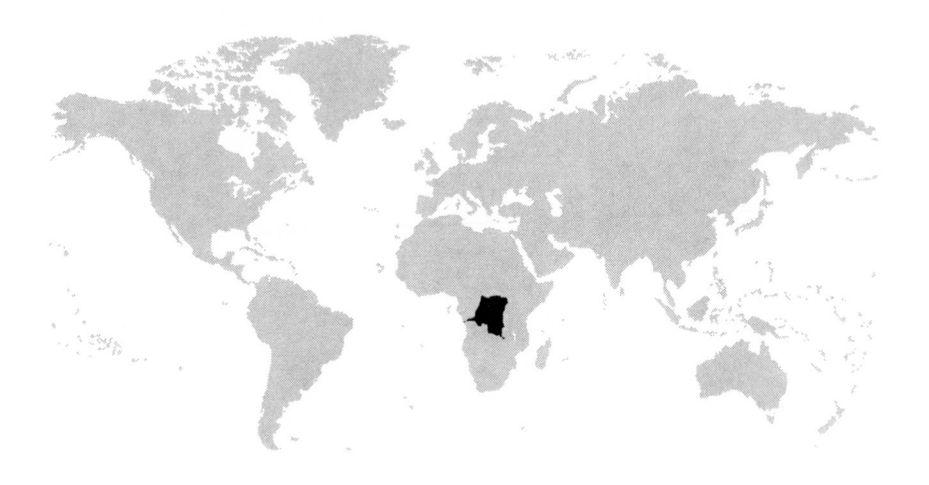

The Democratic Republic of Congo

Since 1998, seventy refugees from the Democratic Republic of the Congo (DRC) have resettled in Minnesota.[53] Congolese refugees flee a long post-colonial history of violence, perpetrated both by governments and warring factions, that has left over two million civilians displaced. The DRC gained its independence from Belgium in 1960.[54]

In addition to internal conflicts, violence and human rights abuses from the 1994 Rwandan genocide spilled over the country's border. In addition, fighting between the government and the Lord's Resistance Army in Uganda has spread to northeastern portions of the DRC. The DRC hosts over 185 thousand refugees from other countries, many of them from the Rwandan and Ugandan conflicts.[55]

French is the official language of the DRC, while many indigenous tribal languages are also spoken. Most Congolese people practice some form of Christianity, while there are groups who practice Islam or indigenous religions. The DRC has a tropical climate, with roughly equal wet and dry seasons.[56]

---

53. MN Department of Health, "Primary Refugee Arrivals to Minnesota."

54. US Department of State, "Democratic Republic of the Congo."

55. US Department of State, "Democratic Republic of the Congo."

56. CIA World Factbook, "Congo, Democratic Republic of the."

Abdul & Dunia:
World Citizens, True Minnesotans

Abdul and his wife, Dunia, tell their story from their house in Minneapolis. They are connected to MCC Refugee Services in a variety of ways. Abdul first came to seek employment through employment services, and later joined the Refugee Speaker's Bureau. Dunia has recently been helping the community health liaison with some special projects around the office. They sit next to each other on a leather couch, sipping Coca-Cola and eating poppy seed Christmas cake from the holiday the weekend prior. They've shooed their four children to the other room to watch television, but they are occasionally still noisy and Dunia gets up to hush them. It is winter, and icicles hang from the roof and the stairs outside. It is a long way from their home in the Congo.

Abdul introduces himself first, his French-African-accented English rolling smoothly off his tongue. He wears dark trousers and a dark polo shirt. His guitar hangs on the living room wall—a sign, he later confirms, that means he is a musician.

"I'm Abdul H. Mali. I'm working currently for the University of Minnesota. I'm called an asylee in the United States for almost four years now. I am coming from—I almost said the United States of America!—coming from the Democratic Republic of Congo, not to be confused with the Republic of Congo, which is a neighbor country to ours. So, like I said, we've been living here for four years. And my spouse and kids just joined me, for a year. But she would rather introduce herself, maybe."

Dunia, her dark African hair woven into braids tight against her head, perches on the edge of the couch cushion. Her bright yellow dress, with bold, colorful paisley shapes, looks like it must have come from Africa.

"My name is Dunia Mali. I've been here for one year and three months, I can say. I came to join my husband. Yeah." Dunia's English is not as fluid as Abdul's, but she speaks with confidence.

Abdul says, "[In the DRC] I was working as a journalist for six years, at the same time I was the representative of the European Union in the base of aviation. I was responsible for their branch in Mbuji Mayi. So I was working with a lot of nongovernmental organizations (NGOs), helping them, carrying them and their goods, and help them operate in the Congo. Major reason being, we don't have many good roads to help all these NGOs circulate and carry out their mission. So, the EU assigned a couple planes back home and I was responsible for that. But my full-time job was as a journalist. Now, as a journalist, I ended up, say, having a contract with the PBS, an American channel. And I helped them to issue two documentaries, political related to some extent. But before we get into those details, I would say my match was pretty much that, working as a journalist.

"I lived in Mbuji Mayi. Mbuji Mayi is pretty much in the center of the Democratic Republic of Congo. It is a place where you have tons of diamonds. It's, once upon a time, called the world capital of diamonds. Most of it was coming from Mbuji Mayi, my home city. So I lived there, but working for the EU and as a journalist I would travel a lot around the country. To the capital city and other small towns and stuff. It was a regular part of my business.

"I met Dunia in 1995, was it?" Abdul asks.

"Three!" Dunia shouts from the other room—she has left to tend to the children.

"Ok, '93. I don't know why I said '95. I met her in 1993, in a choir where she was singing. And I joined. Dunia has been singing ever since she was a little kid. I joined the choir in 1993 and that's where we met. In a Catholic church. So I went to there, we became friends, then we became fiancé, then we got married in 2000. Also, we got married officially—everything was done. We had our first kid the same year, in 2000 in December. So our firstborn is going to just turn ten, actually, this month. So, it's been quite a while."

During the early part of their marriage, Dunia was also busy living life and working.

"I had my—how do you say—my own business. Yes, I was an event planner. Helping people organize weddings, all kinds of events; it may be conferences, it may be music concerts. Also, a kind of, helping people to organize, you know? We didn't have those big rooms in our country. Most of them didn't have enough chairs. They didn't have a kitchen. So when you organize a ceremony, you should know where to find chairs, how to cook, how to help people get settled in there. So that's what I was using with the kind of stuff of mine," Dunia explains.

Abdul starts speaking again, this time about the DRC in general. "The most important thing to know is that the Congo is one of the richest countries in Africa, and probably in the world as well. We have tons of minerals and resources like that. And, like I mentioned before, it's been once upon a time, known as the first producer of diamonds. But we also have copper [and other metals]. The whole story about the war—you know, there has been this war going on in the country for more than ten years now. And it gave way to the killing of nearly six million people. It turned out to be the bloodiest war after the Second World War.

"Put against that, Congo is very poor right now. We have been going through a lot of dictatorship and big disorder going on; catastrophe. Congo is also a place that has become very famous because hundreds of thousands of women have been raped over the course of the ten-year war. And men as well! So, there's a lot of tragic stories in connection with the Congo. This is now, but in the former time as well, because in the colonization of the country by the Belgium, a lot of wrong things happened to the country. Like people having their limbs cut and stuff like that. Huge exploitation. And, yeah—a lot of sad stories about the Congo. Very depressing. We just had the very first so-called democratic election, back in 2006. And it was during this electoral process that I worked in collaboration with PBS.

"In 2006, I got in touch with a team of journalists working for PBS through some acquaintance of mine through the EU. The team of journalists was seeking for a "fixer." This is jargon in journalism. It means a local journalist who's aware of the political situation, the whereabouts, and can connect the foreign or strange media with the local authorities. Not only that, but also help with translation and help people find their way in the country. Fixer. That's what they call them. That's not only in the Congo. It's all over the world. And more and more there's a lot of things being said about fixers that says it's a very risky job. Not only in the Congo, where a couple of them have been killed, which would have been my lot, too, probably," he says this with a laughing voice, but the undertones are grave. "More and more we hear about fixers being murdered or thrown in jail and forgotten about."

Abdul was asked to be a fixer for PBS because of his current job in the local TV and radio media where he used to read the news, he says. The PBS team contacted Abdul in 2006 and asked him to connect them with the appropriate officials and characters for the documentary.

"The first assignment was about the politics in the Congo, in general. I think we mentioned something about the street kids, as well. That one was pretty much a report about the politics. But then, the big one we did later on was like a forty-five-minute one." Abdul sighs, explaining the political themes in the movie. "Our democracy was still very, very young. You could tell how politicians and people would struggle with all these democracy-related terminologies and how you make all these concepts come together. And what does it look like? What you call democracy, something totally different than you guys here in America would think of. It is something just starting. With all the, you know, weaknesses and problems, issues, related to it."

Working as a fixer with an American media company can be dangerous, but Abdul and Dunia were initially not concerned.

Dunia explains, "Actually, you know, it was the first time, and I knew it was a kind of dangerous. But in my country there's something kind of weird, you know. When talking about politics, you can never tell at what time it becomes dangerous. That's why most of people dealing with their routines, dealing with their daily job, find themselves in trouble. That's how it is. If I thought that this is dangerous, I would just"—Dunia's voice drops to a whisper—"'Don't go there!' I couldn't think that it was that dangerous."

Abdul jumps in, elaborating on the situation. "The problem, like she said—you never can tell. There is a semblance of democracy. Sometimes people can say these things on the radio, like question what the president is doing. Because of course all these guys are not serious. Some people have said things and have never really been arrested or threatened. But the major issue is firstly with me, in my case, was my collaboration with external media.

"So while I was doing the job here with my guys, you know, we were wandering all over the place going up and down. Occasionally some of the guys would ask, 'Hey, are you the CIA or what?' But I was kind of used to this kind of thing, working as a journalist. A couple of times I was threatened before, death threatened. My wife received letters and stuff with people menacing me for just saying stuff on the radio. I was just like, 'Ah, this has happened before.'

"Then, one time, when working with the journalists, I remember in the middle of the shootage, this secret service guy came. Of course, they don't wear uniforms, but I noticed him right away.

"They never wear uniforms!" Dunia interjects with indignation.

Abdul continues. "Yah. He was like, 'You must be a CIA!' He looked serious and angry and didn't want our camera guy to continue shooting. I started arguing with that guy; people started gathering around us. And it was done. I didn't take it too seriously. But I think that's about the time the secret service put me on their black list, and probably decided to initiate my arrestation.

"We worked for just one month. But it was pretty intense. We would start at 6:00 a.m. to get back late in the evening. Meaning, people would see you passing in front of their door three, four times a day and it was pretty much remarkable.

"So I believe it was at that time that the secret service started meditating about my case. 'Cause the other thing you need to understand is that back home, if you are not known as working for the power, if you are not defending their point of view on the television or radio, you are somewhat suspicious already. You are potentially somebody who can be used to overthrow the power, or something like that. And what they usually do for most journalists who got killed or thrown in jail, well, they're going to send a bunch of street kids to your house in the middle of the night, break in, and do whatever thing they could do for you. And people will say, 'Ah! He got attacked by street kids,' and that's it. You are dead and forgotten about. You are never going to hear that a huge trial has been organized to establish why somebody got killed.

"When I was doing that documentary, I think two journalists got killed for this. For doing nothing—literally nothing."

Dunia pipes up again. "Can I add something?" Abdul nods, looking at her intently. "There is also something. How do you say? The states, the province where we were living, was politically a kind of red zone for the government. Because years ago, it was kind of, the..."

"The stronghold." Abdul fills in the word for her.

"of opposition to the government," Dunia continues. "So most of the people in that province were against the government. So when they were preparing those elections in 2006, we got more military to enforce the security in Mbuji Mayi. Maybe people would just not go vote, just to boycott the elections. And the government, the president, didn't have a great amount of people in his side, in that province. So wherever they see you with something that doesn't look their colors—you look suspicious. That's where it came from." Dunia nods, finishing her thought.

"And so, it all started like this," Abdul continues. "With little threats on the street, which I probably neglected. I never felt it was very dangerous. But like I always say when I tell this story, I was very intuitive. I think a lot of things happen to me in my life like that. I will feel something. I felt the need I should maybe move. That's what I think. And concurrently, without me really asking for it, a close friend among the colleague journalists invited me to get out of the country for some vacations."

Abdul explains that he had been working on the documentary for a whole month, and even though it was progressing successfully, the work was intense and time consuming. So they took some time off and Abdul went with his coworkers to Minnesota.

This wasn't Abdul's first interaction with people from Minnesota. He had made a connection while learning English.

"How I learned English is another good, long story. I loved English for some reason, ever since I was a little kid. And American English. Of course, back home we also studied bits of English in high school. Just like here, people study French. But you would never be able to speak correctly or fluently English by studying in high school. So what I did, basically, was I memorized songs. I read books. I was pretty much self-trained. And then a very nice history around that is in 1995 I got this tape by"—Abdul pauses, a glimmer in his eye—"Garrison Kiellor! A tape that dated back from 1983, that I got from some missionary that came in the Congo. I was like, *Oh! I would like that tape they are listening with. And it could help improve my understanding of the language, etc.* So I kept it for many, many years, listening to it. Garrison Kiellor. He was from Lake Wobegon, Minnesota, where the...you know. It was pretty much how I came to know English. I learned as an adult." Abdul chuckles warmly. "Yeah."

"One day, quite accidentally, I mentioned it to my PBS coworkers." As Abdul tells the story, Dunia chuckles softly beside him. "I mentioned Lake Wobegon, Minnesota. And people were like, 'What are you talking about? You're talking about Lake Wobegon? You know Lake Wobegon!?' I'm like, 'Yeah, I know Lake Wobegon! I know this guy, Garrison Keillor.' And 'Oh my God! Can't believe this! In the middle of Mbiji Mayi, somebody know Garrison Keillor!'" Abdul's voice squeaks with laughter. "'This is incredible!' And I was like, 'Well, I have a tape of that guy. If you want, I could bring it tomorrow to you.'

"When I brought that tape it was already old, it was super dirty and stuff. They were like, 'Oh my God! Where did you get that?' So then, when I came [to Minnesota], I brought that tape and they take me to Garrison Keillor's show. He looked at that tape, he looked me in the eye, and was like, 'Oh my God! Nineteen eighty-three. *I* don't even have those right now! How did you get this?'" Abdul shakes with laughter. "I just had to tell him the story. He just had to write on the tape, 'Abdul: The

True Minnesotan.'" Dunia and Abdul burst into more gleeful laughter. "Oh, yes, yes, yes. It was pretty much like that."

"So to get back to what I was saying," Abdul says, his voice more serious again. "I had that feeling. I was so, so, so lucky for feeling that and going with my intuition. As soon as I moved to Minnesota, they broke into my house on a Sunday morning." Abdul stops speaking for several seconds.

Abdul explains that the men tried to force his wife to tell them where he was hiding. They searched the house and accused Abdul of being with the CIA. Abdul says they took Dunia to their office and questioned her for hours. Meanwhile, a neighbor called Dunia's father, who got in touch with Abdul. Through the help of his journalist friends, they were able to contact the UN and bring Dunia and the kids to a safe place.

Dunia picks up the story. "We had first to hide. His mother had to hide. My father, too. So it was me, my father, and his mother. We all separated, changed our places a couple times, and then came back." She looks to her husband to continue.

"So...then the UN went to my radio station, tried to find out why they were trying to arrest me," Abdul says. "They sent a lot of agents everywhere, to these secret service places and stuff. First they were like, 'Oh no, nothing. It's not us!' But ultimately, the UN knew that it was them. And the UN got in touch with this arrest warrant that was issued against me. Coming from the high court! You know, saying that I had endangered the country. I had insulted the president. What was the third motive? I can't even remember. So I just looked like some spy in my own country. You know? So the arrest warrant said wherever place they could see me, I should be arrested on the spot.

"And so, after doing that, the UN just called me in Minnesota and said, 'You just can't come back, because we're not able to ensure your safety and security. And we're trying to protect your family, but you need to look for asylum.'

"And so that's how it started another journey for me. From one day to another, I saw everything turned upside down. My career was put to an end quite brutally. And I had to stay in an apartment for almost a year, doing nothing. I had to get those lawyers and stuff. The asylum-seeking process that took almost a year. Huge depression. Not sure of anything. Not sure about safety of my family. Missing my family, of course. And it was just so terrible. So terrible. Terrible two years."

Meanwhile, Dunia was back in the DRC. She struggles to say what it was like. "A kind of...how do you say?" Dunia says a word in French. Abdul translates. "A void."

"Yes, a void," Dunia agrees. "An emptiness. You know? When he left, it was about to go for one month or three weeks. I don't even remember. I had my last one who was only one week when he left. So the eldest one was about to begin elementary school. He was six years old. The second one had to go to kindergarten. And I was there. When he was there, I could work, but I know that he was there we were helping each other. But when he left, it was like, what am I going to do? I had most of important things in my house taken away when they came and said, 'We are searching for proof of his betrayal.' So they took most of important things. They took the car. They took all his...journalist stuff we had." Dunia searches for the word and speaks in French to her husband.

"Yeah, all my equipment," Abdul explains.

"All his equipment, they took that. How could I begin again? So it was very tough. The kids were asking, 'Where is Dad? When is he coming back?' Was he staying forever? Do I stay here forever? Am I safe enough, with the kids? How long should I stay with this kind of unsafe state? So it was really, really hard.

"And when I've been questioned by those people. You know, they take you for hours. Questioning you the same questions." Dunia's voice becomre more agitated. "I had my baby. You know, in my country, we don't feed by bottles when the baby is still too little. We just feed by...breast. They take your baby in the other room, and you are listening to him crying! So your baby is there crying and you are answering those silly questions. And they are menacing you. 'You're never going to back outside again!' It was stressful." Dunia stops her part of the story, turning it back over to Abdul.

"All of this happened. Even menacing to rape her. And I'm here [in

Minnesota], and I'm hearing all of that." Abdul's voice is quiet now, almost weary. "And not sure of anything. I was going to go crazy that first year. I was so depressed. I was touched deeply, deeply abused. And then I get here, of course I was speaking a little English, but I'm not able to work as a journalist. This is a very competitive thing. And working as a journalist, your language skills have to be above the average. You have to be able to speak better than the average person. And I was not reaching the average person in language! So I saw my career completely torn apart. So what am I going to do now? Going back to school, how is that even going to be possible? I didn't have any means. My friends were helping me with food and clothing and lodging. Where am I going to get all the money to get my family here? How long is that going to take? You constantly live in, you know, worry. Every minute of your life is about worry."

Abdul's journalist friends from PBS had helped him find an apartment and would visit occasionally, taking Abdul out to restaurants and such.

"They were helpful. But still, that's not enough to help cover all the problems you face out of here," Abdul says. "I got connected with MCC after I was actually granted my asylum. Because I worked with the Advocates for Human Rights. At that time they were called Minnesota Advocates for Human Rights. They are the ones who referred me to MCC. After I was granted asylum, then I was at least able to look for a job at that time. So they connected me there and they also helped me very much. It was a place where I could express myself and discuss with people. And of course, they show you the way, you know.

"This is one of the toughest things to achieve when you arrive here. Especially for people arriving from different countries from Africa. Everything is different, including the culture, the environment. Everything is different! You have to learn every little thing. You're like a baby, pretty much. You're like a baby.

"It's not like you're going to go on the street and ask everybody, 'Can you show me how to do this?' People are so busy! They work fast; they walk fast. Well, you feel that it's not appropriate to stop everybody. Everything is just in a constant motion.

"[The Advocates] was a good place. You meet, you share your story.

There was a time...every time I told my story, and it still comes a little bit again, I would kind of sink into depression again. I would feel all the pain surfacing again. The more I did it, the more it helped me to take out this anger and all this fears and stuff. Even when I almost became sure that my family was going to come here, I was still not myself. Even when they got here! Occasionally, I have all these bad dreams. Like I dream that I was arrested and I mean, I say, 'Oh, I thought I had got out of this country! I was away! What's happening?' Then you wake up and realize you were just dreaming. It's happened many times. It was intense. I realized every day that I would have been dead when I heard about a lot of journalists who were killed for literally nothing!"

Things eventually did get better for Abdul.

"The first thing was when I was granted asylum. I was not really prepared for that. I didn't even know if it was going to be possible. It was like, if I am denied asylum, what am I going to do? What's the next step? Am I going to go in Europe? Am I going to go in Africa? Where? How am I going to start that? You know?

"When I got asylum, that was the first time that I felt like, 'Well, at least I'm sure that I can, for a couple years at least, be here and make sure I get my family out of that place.' You know? That was the first major step. Of course, following that I got the first job. At least I was able to send them something."

"My first job, I was a customer service representative, yeah, at a financial institution. In Eden Prairie. I worked as a bilingual customer service representative. And then, I got the job from the University of Minnesota where I have been working for the past three years as an audio-visual technician. I like it, because it's not that stressful for me. It's pretty much the small things I was doing as a journalist. Connecting cables, cameras, working on mixing boards, setting projectors, working with a bunch of students I supervise. Yeah. It's kind of an easy job. And less stressful for me. But you know, I'm always thinking that sometime I might step back on my career at some point and maybe continue. Maybe with a different drift, but being in my career, definitely. You know, I'm working on that."

Before Dunia came to Minnesota, she lived in fear and uncertainty.

"You know, it was a kind of danger for me. I had kids that had a father, or they should. They had the right to live with their father. But staying like we stayed in the country. At the beginning—I didn't tell you—a couple times we couldn't talk even by phone. So when I was hiding, and how can you tell the kids that first it was, 'When is Dad going to be back?' and I was like, 'Yes, he is going to be back.' 'But when? And where is he?' And we wouldn't talk with them. 'So is he dead?' 'No, he's not dead.' It was strange. Even my last one didn't know what his father was like. He was calling the cell phone Papa Abdul. He didn't know it was someone, a real person existed.

"So I was—it was a great thing that could happen to me at that time. That they could get back to their father. Also for myself—we couldn't stay like that. I'm here and he's there. It didn't make sense. It was kind of restarting life. And also we all the time that we stayed back home in the country, if they know that he's there, the same place where the people who worked with, they may seek me again! I was just like, 'It may begin again. They may call me again! They may call again. You don't live your life. You don't...you don't feel yourself safe with your own parents.' Something like that. You're kind of...out of your mind. It's a crazy thing. So that's something I can never wish to happen to someone else. It was really bad. If you don't feel yourself safe in your own country, that's something very bad."

Abdul was in Minnesota for three long years before his family was able to join him. "They've only been here for a year. They actually got here in early September [2009]."

Dunia says she feels safer in Minnesota, but it is hard to forget her family back home. Her siblings, parents, and in-laws are all back in the DRC, and it is impossible to know if they are in danger of being interrogated or threatened again by the people seeking Abdul.

Now that Dunia, Abdul, and the children are together in Minnesota, they are learning what it means to rebuild their lives. Part of this is adjusting to a new culture and choosing what aspects of their own culture to retain, and what to let fade away.

"I think the hardest thing that I probably miss is the warmth, you know?" Abdul begins, "In America, people seem to be very busy. And really concerned about themselves. You know, it's this individualism has reached a certain point which is striking when you first show up in America. There's not a lot of contact between people. People are only open to you when, like, you show up, there's a problem, or in a certain environment. But you can't allow yourself, on the street, to touch somebody on the shoulder. 'Hey! How come you touch me?' You never hear that in Africa!"

As Abdul speaks, Dunia chuckles. "Because it's totally normal that somebody touches you." They both are laughing now. "It's so normal! It's like a little detail, but quite meaningful. You know? People are very warm in Africa."

"And then this weather. This weather. Oh, my God. Having been born under the equator, and having grown up there every day you have big sun. You sweat. And suddenly, you are trapped in the middle of an apartment or a house. Just imagine for the first three years I was here, I didn't have a car. I would just walk, because every little money I had had to be spared." Abdul sighs deeply.

In terms of preserving culture for their children, Abdul hopes to teach them respect for their elders.

"In Africa, there is a hierarchy distance, as Malcom Gladwell calls it in the *Outliers*, the fact that in Africa there is a lot of respect for seniors and elders, you know. There is a lot of that. In America, maybe, you have to control very much what you are telling a kid pretty much like you would with an adult! You just feel like they can talk to you sometimes how they want." Abdul laughs incredulously. "But at the same time, I want them to be open. Because the backside of a lot of respect is it will probably make people not able to express themselves. In case you find an adult or a senior being wrong, you just can't tell because they are a senior. I think that is not correct, too. That is not good. So, probably, let's go half way."

"Can I add something?" Dunia interjects, "I think, also in our traditions around weddings and marriage. That's—I don't feel at all here. Like, how people can get married. The families just don't meet [in my culture], but they exchange."

"Can I say something on that?" Abdul asks.

"He can explain better than me!" says Dunia.

"People are so connected. And marriage is considered to be a vital thing in life. And kids, as well. When you marry, you don't marry for yourself. That's probably what I would like to emphasize. In America, sometimes our impression is that mostly it is about the guy and the girl who are getting married. Of course the parents are informed, they can say something, but it's not really their business. If you want to just jump, you jump, with whatever a person you want to. And that's totally your life. But it's not like that in Africa. In Africa, marriage is about everybody. It's about the uncle as well. Everybody can say something on it. They keep an eye on you. If somebody is going astray, they will intervene and advise you. They will tell you how to live.

"I hope that [my children] will really take the time to think twice whenever they have chosen somebody. That's going to be it. They will make the choice once and for the good. And they need to make sure they will keep their wives forever. They have to be prepared so that whenever problems arise in their house, in the marriage, they will be able to work them out."

As to whether they want their children to marry within their own culture, "That..." Abdul sighs. "That, I will still give them some freedom, you know. I will advise. I really hope they will do the best thing, but it's not like I will be running behind them to tell them, 'Here's the person you have to choose.'

"The way I deal with my kids, I tell them back on the eve of Christmas. We sat here, we prayed together. I said, 'Find friends everywhere. Among white people. Among Chinese people. Among, uh, whatever. Latinos, whatever. All of these people are beauties! Look at them as beauties. They are flowers. That's what I see when I look at white people. I find them beautiful. And I glorify God. I see how much God is, how big God is. And I mean, it's beautiful to see this! And when you—when you look at the world in this perspective, you're never going to be judgmental. Or feel like, when somebody says something wrong to you, they have said it because you are black. No! You have to be able to interpret that they have done this or said this because they are mad. Because that's normal.

Somebody from your own race can say the same thing to you."

Abdul says, "Of course, I might have the tendency to be slow when I use the computer—because I only start using it now! You've been using it ever since you were eight years old. Well, it's normal!" Abdul is speaking loudly, but with a big smile on his face and Dunia giggles beside him. "It's normal, you know? My kids won't be acting like Africans. Look, they can speak English now, and they've only been here for one year. They understand that I write music, and my kid was there last night, literally correcting me, when I made a little mistake; he saw it immediately. I mean, he's ten years old. Tell me how much is he going to know these things in three years or when he is going to be twenty-five. He's going to be completely different. Completely different. So that's the way we train our kids. We want them to be citizens of the world. And see the beauty displayed throughout the universe by diversity. Open their eyes to see the beauty. Not to see boundaries or limitations."

Abdul's voice takes on a teasing tone. "Did you even choose to be black or to be white? If I had known, I would never have chosen to be born in Africa! And to be hunted down by some militia, whatever it is. You know?" The mirth fades from his voice as he becomes serious. "I just didn't have a choice."

"Well! So, I really—I'm working day and night. I'm so blessed that my wife sees the world the same way as me. And so I think, our kids have all the chances to grow as citizens of the world. Especially now that I am living here. I feel safer in a stranger country! I feel safer in a stranger country! I can't think of going back. If they are to tell me to go back today, I'll go like, 'Hell no!' You know?" Abdul pauses for a beat. "How's that? How much do you think I'm still bound to that country? Just because my siblings are there, my family, my family-in-law. But if there was nobody from my surroundings, I would have forgotten about it." Abdul breathes in, pausing even longer.

Abdul moves on now to talk about his experience on the Refugee Speaker's Bureau.

"Like I said before, I decided to do it as a way to free all depression and tension I had accumulated as a result of going through these sad experiences. Although at times I remember, a couple times, probably three times or four, I just stopped in the middle of my speech and couldn't speak anymore. I felt like crying. I felt completely invaded, overwhelmed by sad feelings and stuff. And I stopped. But I think over the course of time I have become more able to freely talk about it, and it's almost becoming, you know, an old story to some extent. So it's been helpful for me to talk about that. And of course, I used to talk a lot as a journalist. These are the only ways I could express myself.

"And of course, it also helped me evaluate my capacity to communicate in my English. To see if people could actually understand me or not! Every time I spoke, for example, I would ask, 'Have you been able to understand me?' And overwhelmingly people would say, 'Oh, yeah! We can still tell you are not an American native, but your English is still understandable.' That's very good for me. It gives me hope. Sometimes I might get back on my career like journalism. I like journalism! I like talking on the radio, man!"

Dunia laughs again at her husband and speaks again. "Maybe one little thing…is that another thing I love about America is that, the kind of diversity. Do you say diversity? That kind of diversity that makes, in a certain way, a kind of unity." Her voice betrays a sense of awe in this idea. "There's so much people coming from all over the world that makes the nation, and to me it's a kind of amazing. In my country we are all black with different tribes. But it is difficult to make that kind of united nation, back home. And that's it here—why? How? It's kind of amazing for me. That's what I really like here. It will help me one day go back home and know how to manage people beyond their differences. And to get a better country."

"And I will build on that," Abdul says. "It's not only what I want to preserve. There are of course a lot of good values here, not to talk about opportunities as well. I feel like America is a place where you can undertake your own business; as long as you respect the rules and pay your taxes you are good to go. You can do it. You won't see anybody trying to get in your way, forcibly. There are so many openings we don't have back home, of course. You feel free. The opportunities are immense.

I would sit any time at my bench to write music, I know there is always going to be lights, power. There is going to be water on the tap. You have a certainty for certain things you don't have back home or in other parts of the world.

"In general, I think we feel very good and I'm very happy for my kids. Especially they can go to grade school and study. I hope they can evolve very well. I have some smart boys. I want them to push hard and get ahead and become real guys. This is something great. This is something great."

Iraq

Instability for many of Iraq's civilians started with the launch of the Iran–Iraq War in 1980, an eight-year conflict that resulted in a stalemate. Three years later, war came again to Iraq with the launch of the Persian Gulf War, a conflict that began with the Iraqi invasion of Kuwait. War again broke out in Iraq with the 2003 US-led invasion. These wars, combined with the brutal dictatorship of Saddam Hussein, have left over three and a half million Iraqis displaced.[57]

Of the Iraqis who fled, many sought asylum in the neighboring countries of Syria and Jordan.[58] These countries, similar to Iraq, have expansive deserts and dry, hot summers. Most Iraqi refugees are Muslims, although Iraq also has a small Christian population. The official language of Iraq is Arabic, while Kurdish is spoken by the Kurds, an ethnic group comprising approximately 15 percent of the population.[59]

Some Iraqi refugees have returned to their areas of origin, while others have attempted to integrate into other Arab countries. The United States first accepted Iraqi refugees in the aftermath of the Gulf War,[60] and so far 335 Iraqis have resettled in Minnesota.[61]

---

57. UNHCR.org, "Iraq."

58. Center for Applied Linguistics, "Refugees from Iraq."

59. CIA World Factbook, "Iraq."

60. Center for Applied Linguistics, "Refugees from Iraq."

61. Minnesota Department of Health, "Primary Refugee Arrivals to Minnesota."

Senan:
Self-Starter, Cross-Cultural Navigator

This story comes from Senan, a program specialist in refugee resettlement and placement at MCC Refugee Services. For his casual-Friday work attire, Senan wears jeans, a gray hooded sweatshirt, and a stocking cap pulled down to his thick eyebrows. He tells his story in the MCC office's "living room," a small space with comfortable chairs and a couch. Senan eases into his chair, relaxed and ready to begin speaking. Senan has told his story to MCC staff before, and whoever hears it is left marveling at what he went through to get here. He begins with his childhood, rattling off the details of his life in a detached manner, as if he had told this story many times before.

"I was born in the south of Iraq; it's Basrah. I was born with eight years of war with Iraq and Iran. There's a war, but we still go to school and I follow an education from city to city. Like, we went to the middle of Iraq for I think three or four months. It became very dangerous there and they keeping shooting rockets in the south of Iraq. And we decide to move to the middle, just for three months and go back." Senan's voice gets quieter. "We went there also following the schools, and after that, went back to the south of Iraq; it's Basrah again. And start studying again.

"My father is an accountant at the University in Basrah. He is always taking me with him, like if I have a holiday or something, I go with him, watch him, how he do his work and stuff. It's fun to go there when we kids were young. He retired after that in the 1989? Yeah, 1989. He retired, because they start pushing him. If you are a manager of all accountants

124

in the university, you have to be in the Baath party, and he don't like the Baath party and he decide to just quit or retire. He retired, and after that, we start spending the retired money. They give us like three thousand dinar. Three thousand dinar is like fifty [US] dollar a month.

"If you want to buy a cigarette, a cigarette is fifty dinar; it mean six pack of cigarettes, your money is done for the month. And you have to find yourself some kind of job or something to get that money. We have three trees in our house—it's for fruit, and those fruit is very special. It's not here. It's not a date plum or something. It looks like a date, but it's not date. And we start like, every season, every summer, we cook with all this fruit from these trees and we sell it in the market.

"We have just three trees, but they are big, like thick. They make more than five hundred kilo of fruit, yeah.

"We keep the fruit and sell it, and just keep that money to go through the winter and same again with the next summer until the 1995. Because in the 1995, between the 1991 and 1995, we went through the war with Kuwait and the power was shut off for three years and they didn't fix it. They fix it again after the two year, but it's come like two hours in the day or three hours. And that is the machines for the building.

"The sewers is not working and the sewers start coming up and up and up and up and killed the trees. It killed all the trees in our house and not just our house: most of the houses, just—it just disappeared because of the sewer coming out and finish everything. Yeah, we thought that we have to look for another job. I am in the high school in these years.

"I decide, I'm good with electrician stuff. So I start fixing some things for the neighbors and they give me money. One day, one guy just came to me, he said, 'I bring you a big generator. Put it in your house and you sell power for the neighborhood because we don't have no power.' And I tell him it's a good idea; he give me rent for the space and a salary to maintain the machine and watch the breakers. When it's stripped, you have to pull it back. And it's a very hard job. It's noisy and there's a lot of oils and gas and diesel and everything."

Senan kept the machine in the garden of his family's home, where he lived with his parents, his elder sister, his pharmacist brother, and younger brother. Even though the generator was noisy, Senan's family decided to keep it because it brought in an income, about seventy-five thousand dinar each month.

"We worked with it like two years and two years I didn't leave the house, just stay there, because I know if I leave, my dad—he don't know how to use this machine; my other brothers don't know what's going on; and if I leave it, it's just—something is going to happen.

"One day, my friends came to me and said, 'Just one day, just one hour, just go outside with us just to have fun, buy some clothes and coming back.' I said, 'Okay, we can do it.' It's like 4:30 in the evening and we went to the market to buy some clothes and eat and do stuff and go back to the house. And when I went back to the house"—Senan's voice raises in pitch, with heightened excitement and a hint of amusement—"I saw a fire coming from my house!

"Because my dad, he don't know how to turn [the generator] on and he didn't change something he was supposed to change before he start the machine. He give power to the grid and not to the people. And if you give power to the grid, it mean you are giving the power for the whole neighborhood. And the engine is too small to give that much power and it just—he just burn it." Senan laughs. "And its cost me a lot of money, too, 'cause the guy, he said 'You are responsible for it. You have to be there and you left it there.'"

The owner of the generator fixed it, and then kept Senan's salary until it paid for the repairs. Senan says that in 1995 or 1996, the man decided to finish the contract and took the machine away. So Senan decided to learn how to fix air conditioners from a friend, and for two years he was paid to fix the neighbors' air conditioners.

And then, in 1998, Senan's brother was arrested, along with some other students, by Saddam Hussein's police. He was in jail for two years.

"We don't know where my brother is and we are all scared."

And he was scared of something else. Senan explains that women are often arrested to make prisoners talk—and the technique was often effective, pressuring prisoners to say just about anything. "Anything—just to release your sister or release your wife from where you are seeing now, because they abuse them or doing something in front of you."

So Senan, afraid for his sister's well being, brought her to Baghad to protect her, and they lived there for two years before hearing from his brother.

"We hear that my brother he is in a big jail in Baghdad and he call us and he say, 'I am there in this jail after this two years.' They killed all the friends with him except just him and three or four guys. They are lifetime in prison. He said just bring me my books and stuff. He started studying there in that jail, just for fun.

"In 2002, when the war happen, when the Americans come and they open the jail, he just went out from the jail." Senan's voice gets quieter and slower as he explains what had happened to his brother.

"They said [my brother was in] some kind of group who was doing communication with Iranians and stuff, but there's nothing like that. They come and pick up one, like they take you to the security office and they start hitting you, like with machines and stuff. They make you talk. And some time you don't have anything to talk about and they ask you for names. You don't have no names." Senan's words spill out at quickening pace. "But because of the pain, you start to say anything.

"But if you say one name, they hit you for the second and they hit you for the third. Some guy, they just took him and he remember all his friends and brought everybody from there, from the college." Senan laughs in disbelief. "Who knows if that's why they brought them there. We come visit him after two years; he's skinny. He's still with the same pants after two years, but he roll it two times, because when he went he's 250 pounds; now he's 100 and it's too big for him."

Senan's brother started studying officially again in 2002, when the war freed him from the jail, and he soon finished college and became a pharmacist.

"After the 2002, I have an experience with an electrician. I studying electrician, and I became very good with electricity and stuff and I became very good at electrician. I went to the US embassy and they have a company called KBR. It works with Halliburton. They test me and they hire me as an electrician and interpreter with the US embassy. I worked there since like 2002; October 19 or 15, I start working there."

When the US invaded Iraq, the Americans took over one of Saddam Hussein's palaces as an embassy.

"And I enjoyed my work. I went from an electrician to a foreman. I supervised like four Iraqi guys, and after that they became six and I'm supervising six Iraqi guys and I'm being supervise by an American supervisor. And we did a lot. We build like six or seven camps there at the palace. We did services to the palace, to the embassy, to everything there inside the palace.

Senan explains that he liked his job and his coworkers like him, too. He was making good money and getting professional experience with a US company. But one day, Senan had no choice but to quit.

"One day, I'm walking to work and somebody walked behind me, and he said my name. Like if you are walking down the street and somebody say your name, you turn to see who is this guy. I turn and I don't know him and he said, 'Are you Senan?' He said, 'Did you come yesterday to my house? To buy my car?' I say, 'No, I didn't come to your house.' And he said, "Yeah, they say somebody from here is named Senan and you work here and came to my wife.' And I say no. [I say,] 'I'm not him. I already have a car.' And he just said, 'Oh, sorry. Thank you.'

Senan says that the man must have just wanted to identify him so he would be able to match his face with his name.

"I went inside [my work] and I heard the news inside that workers are saying, like something happened, and I say, 'What's going on?' And they said, that there is a big news. Just, 'You don't see the letters outside?' I said no. They said, 'There's a letter saying if you work today not tomorrow, if you don't quit today, you get killed.' And I said, 'There's somebody just ask me my name and he did this and this to me, and he stranger. I don't know him.' They say, 'He is one of them.'

"And after three hours, I didn't decide to quit, and they say that militia, they are outside with guns, waiting for us just to go out. And the military inside, there's a—there's a military group there. They heard about it and they take like Humvees and tanks outside, and there's snipers sitting out there and they push them very far from the palace, just to let us go out from another way. It's a very hard day. And they start shooting between the British and the American soldiers and them till they became very safe for us and they let us go."

So Senan quit his job that day, and left with a certificate proving he had worked there and a promise that his salary was on the way.

"After three, four months, I open a shop for me. I say, it's just—maybe they just forgot about us because we just quit. And I open my shop, and sitting there and do stuff, doing air conditioning jobs and heat and stuff and cars come in to fix the ACs. I did a good job. Like six months I'm working and getting money."

One day, when Senan was closing the shop for the day, he heard from two friends that one of his friends, a neighbor, had been killed.

"And I took my car and go there—there, and I saw him laying down in the street. He just got killed. And we sit there for three days. It's like, we do like—it's just like, in Iraq, if somebody die, they do three days there at his house sitting there and read the Koran and stuff. But I talk to my father, I said 'Okay, they killed my friend probably they are going to come and kill me,' and stuff like that."

Senan's father told him not worry about it—he was just being paranoid after seeing his friend killed.

"And after one week had gone, I saw somebody watching me. I see him; he's just watching me. Everywhere I go, I see him in front of me. I tell my father, he say, 'No, he's just crazy. Everybody know he's crazy.' I tell him, 'No, but he's all the time after me, just watching me, where I go, what I dress, what I'm driving. Every time I go to the market, it's far away, like one hour driving, and he's there.' He said, 'Ah, probably not.'

"I told one of my friends, I told him 'Okay, let's walk there in the street and you go left, I go right, and let's see where he go.' And he came after me and he start watching me and I said, 'That's it; he's coming after me,' and when I went back to him, there's a new car just coming to pick him up because they knew I was after him and they come and pick him up.

"I told my brother—my father and brother, they say, 'They are not going to do anything to you if you are inside the house.'"

One day, Senan's friends came to visit him at his home. "We are sitting outside in the street, just in front of my gate and we saw a white SUV just out in from of me. I said, 'I don't know anybody with this kind of car, a new car.' And we know this car is the specific for militia or the government."

Senan didn't know what to do. If he ran and it was nothing, his friends could just laugh and explain that he was running for no reason. But if this was the militia, running could cause them to open fire.

"I'm sitting like almost to the ground. I did like I was going to jump, and he stop. 'I said stop.' And he start shooting like bad words, like something like that: 'Stop.' And I didn't stop. He just pull his gun and shoot one time; he hit the wall; and I'm lucky that front gate is open, because my dad, everyone who go out, he come and close the door with that bar. It's like one three feets long. He—I lock it to be nobody open the door and this day he didn't close the door. And, uh, I run and he shoot the door— the front gate—and he come after me our house is 450 meters square. It's like too big, and our house is all in the back of that, of that 440, and, uh, the front, it's all like a big garden. And I didn't run straight in the garage. I run curve in the garden to be if he want to shoot me, he cannot just shoot me 'cause I'm going like left and right and stuff. And I went behind my house. They thought I enter to the house, but I didn't enter to the house, so I don't lock myself inside. And he shoot three times, like after me in the garden, but he didn't touch me."

Three men were chasing him on foot, and one drove the SUV.

"The driver, he have a gun also but he's facing to my friends outside, but they don't move; they just stay there and three chasing me. One, he come from the left; one, he come from the right; one, he stayed just in the front gate. There's some kind of sand in the back of my house—I slipped in it, and I slapped my face in the ground, because I'm just scared from running. And he almost come and get me. It's too close to me, but he thought I enter to the house and didn't see me laying in the ground."

Senan ran to the neighbor's house, but they wouldn't let him in because they were afraid of what could happen to them.

"I jump to the end of their house; the lady, she don't know me and she's cooking the dinner. It's almost like seven o'clock. It's dark and she saw me jumping in the house. She thought I'm thief and she start screaming and they know. When she start screaming, they know it's this house, and they come after me. I hide in a tree and they just pass me and then went behind this house."

So Senan went to the next house and was finally given a hiding place, under their bed.

"She moved her bed and she tell me to lay down under the bed and she just put the bed back. She tell me, 'What do you want?' and I tell her, 'I want a gun and I want water.' She brought me a water first and she brought me a gun from the house."

Senan told her to close all the doors and lock them—if anybody came to the house, call him on his cell phone so he can be prepare to shoot.

"And she brought me a bottle of water like this big." Senan draws a line from the inside of his elbow to the tip of his hand. "It's too long."

"I couldn't open the cap and drink the water, because it's hitting the bed from the top. I just open the cup a little bit and push it and take some swig from it and I thought, 'Okay, I'm dropping some water and if they see the water under the bed, they will know I'm here.' But I am breathing very hard because I was running. I'm breathing very hard and if they don't see the water, they will hear my breath."

Fifteen minutes later, Senan's assailants left to drive around the neighborhood to watch for him. So Senan called his cousins and asked them to come visit the family of his friend who had recently been killed—that way, their visit would not be suspected as a get-away scheme for Senan. Senan told his cousins to park their car in the garage so he could sneak in and they could drive him away to safety without suspicion.

"They come after one hour. I jump in the car and we went far away from the city. Like, two hour driving, but somebody just tell them the plate number and they said that and they follow us. We know a big family there in the road. We told them they are coming to kill me and they stop them in the road with guns and stuff.

"I went like two hours driving. All this time, I'm not believing I'm still alive because of what happened."

Senan says that as he was being driven to safety, he began to have a flashback to earlier that day when he was almost shot from two or three meters away. And he began reflecting on the violence in the rest of his city.

"Nobody escaped from them in Basrah. They killed a lot of interpreters that worked with the company, a lot of laborers and everything. Nobody escaped, you can just go to the Internet and just say any words, and they are going to give a story about people who got killed there in Basrah who worked with United State companies. Nobody can keep from them, because they are trained. When they come for you, they took pills so they cannot feel; they don't remember they killed anything. These pills, I think, are used for hysteria or if you have mental health. That's the pills they take and they go out and kill people. They dress up in suits, they dress up nice: suits, black suits and stuff. They are very tall and they choose people who have muscles and stuff.

"We just continue driving until I get to a farm; it's for our family. I stay there and they give me a gun, just to make me feel better. I said I cannot forget. It's just...scary.

"We stay at the farm for fifteen days. My brother the pharmacist got me a passport and a new ID and stuff. After the fifteen days, they got a ticket for me to go to Syria.

"From there I fly to Syria and stay there for three years and a half. The militia knows I am there in Syria and they knows that my brother did the passport for me and they put an envelope with a letter saying, 'We going to kill you,' with seven bullets. Each bullet is for one of the family. After the threat, Senan's brother decided to follow him from Iraq to Syria.

"And he came there, stayed with me with all his family—the wife and his kids—and stayed there. And after that, he heard that they came to his pharmacy and they burn it all. They put a fire in it and they just burn it all and he just got very, very upset because he lost the only thing he got in his life."

Senan's brother decided to leave Syria and go to Baghdad, rather than home to Basrah. His wife went back to Basrah, however, and lived in a different house than the one in which they had previously lived. She had decided to wait for the time her husband could return and rebuild their life. Two years later, he heard that a military had come and pushed the militia from the south of Iraq. No longer fearing his life, Senan's brother returned to Basrah and rebuilt his pharmacy—this time with a security camera.

"It look nice. He send me pictures when I am in Syria. And one day I'm here also [I] heard that my dad was visiting my pharmacist brother with my small brother. My brother and a consultant was going to eat lunch because he was hungry. They go across the street and they took the corner and there's a car bomb that in the front of the pharmacy and they burn it again! I have a picture of my brother there in the pharmacy when it's just black—nothing there. And they have the pictures before it's burned and after it's burned. It's a big loss. It's like a thousand of dollars just gone.

"Now he don't have no pharmacy. He just say 'I'm quit. I'm not going to do it again.' Because he lost money and almost lost his life and my brother and my father, also.

"In Damascus I applied for the IOM; it's in United Nation and they give you a bed and pillow and they tell you go ahead and find your house or apartment; we aren't going to help you with anything more. You have to sit there and somebody help you from your country. My dad send me three hundred every month just to go through the month and pay my bills and everything."

Senan says his passport was stamped when he entered Syria, which meant he was unable to work in that country. If somebody catches you working, you could be deported, Senan says. Each month, Senan had to go to the immigration office to have his passport restamped. In order to get passports stamped, people commonly bribed immigration officers with the equivalent of twenty or thirty dollars—otherwise, they risked deportation. Immigration police also frequently check people's documents in their homes to make sure they had been stamped. Senan explains that his money for the bribes came from his family back in Iraq. They wanted to join Senan in Syria, but it was not possible.

"If they come all to Syria, nobody can support us. We supposed to have someone support us there."

Senan explains that the only way for a person to apply for refugee status was to come to Syria, unless the person could prove he worked with the United States—then he could go to the IOM office in Iraq.

"One day, I thought about something, like, 'okay; I have friends in United States. His name is Randy and he opened a Yahoo email for me, and when he opened it for me he said, 'You know this folder; this folder is has all my information: my phone, my address in United States. If something happen and you want to come to the United States, you're free to come to visit.' And I thought about it...."

So Senan emailed Randy, his former supervisor at the US embassy. He explained everything that happened to him, how he was forced to quit his job for fear of being killed and that he had fled from Iraq to Syria.

"He said, 'Anything I can do for you?' I tell him to just write me a letter that supports me in here, because they don't trust that I'm working with United States. He send me a letter in the same time I went to the IOM. I'm saying 'Okay, I'm working with United States.' Before I'm afraid to say that, because in Syria, its Baath party, also. That time I went there and talk to them and they said 'We want interpreter.' I said, 'I don't want interpreter, because I have some information I don't want anybody to know.'"

The interpreter was asked to leave, and Senan explained in English what had happened to him, where he had worked, and where he hoped to go.

"I believe that there's a visa for us just to go to the United States just to become safe," Senan told an administrator.

"She said, 'Yeah, we can help you.' She did the process within nine months. I finish all the processing with IOM and I flew to here. My US tie here in the United States is Randy. I lived with him for almost two years in his house, not paying anything; no rent."

Senan came as a refugee to Minnesota through the MCC, but his experience was unique because of his language abilities.

"I think I'm different than other refugees, because first when I came here, I speak English and know a little bit about the culture. Because it's three years working with the United States and know how they work, how they feel, how they talk, and everything.

"But you have to apply for Social Security card, ID, and driver's license. You have to go buy all this paperwork and bank account, the overdraft or something if you go over the zero and stuff. You don't know that. I was just confused and confused and confused, and scared to go out, also, because I don't know the roads; it's too confusing for me. Every time I want to buy something or go to the market, I call Randy to come pick me up and take me to this market. If it's close, I tell him to come and pick me up because I scared to go there and not coming back here."

Senan started looking for a job, but before he found one, the director of case management services at MCC called him to let him know there was a job opening at MCC. Senan explains that he filled out an application via email and went into the office to complete a computer test. Senan was offered the job. On October 1, 2009, six months after arriving in the United States, Senan had a job in MCC's refugee resettlement program.

"It's been a good experience working here. I know more about different cultures, like Somalis and the Karen—everything. I didn't know about those cultures. And also you have that power to work with your same culture, with Iraqis. I know who is coming and who is not coming. It is nice. And people come to the office.

"I tell the staff every time in the meeting, 'You are my family. I don't have no family here.' All the time when I have good news or bad news, I bring it to the office, because I am talking to somebody who cared about it."

Senan was in Minnesota for almost a year when he became friends with another Iraqi man who was from the same part of Iraq. They had enough in common to become fast friends, even to the point of his friend sharing his family.

"They are a good family; they really like me. Day after day when I go visit them, they don't want me to go back to Randy. They say, 'We don't eat the same as he eats. We'll cook for you, you just stay here.' They kept begging me to stay there. And then one night or two nights, I started staying there. Sometime one week. And when I say, 'I'm going home.' They started crying, 'No, don't leave! Don't go. We start loving you. We don't want you to go.'

"One day they, they have two girls. I said, 'Why am I just sitting with them? Why don't I start building my own house? Have a wife and kids and stuff.' And they are a good family. I asked the mom if she could talk with her daughter and say that I want her to be my wife. She talked with her, and she said yes. And after that, I talked to the brother and the brother said, 'I'm okay with you, but you have to have your own apartment and stuff.' And I was okay with that; it's not a big thing to do.

So Senan, the brother, and another Iraqi man got dressed up and went to speak with the father.

"He said, 'You are a good man. I feel safe about my daughter with you.' And I said okay. We did the engagement this day. I went the same day to buy all the rings and all the gold for her. We did the engagement at one o'clock in the morning."

The Imam came to the house and performed the formal engagement ceremony.

"And I came back to work the next day and I talked with Rachele [director of Refugee Services] in the morning when I came to the office, and she was just surprised. I didn't want to tell people via email. She said, 'No way! You're not going to say it via email. We'll have a special meeting.' So she sent a confusing email about a meeting and I tell everybody here."

Not sure why the meeting had been called, the entire twenty-two-person staff gathered in a meeting room, nervously waiting for the announcement. Had somebody died? Had they been awarded a grant for a new program? Senan made his announcement, shocking the staff into a stunned silence—and then congratulations and smiles surrounded Senan.

"And after one month, I think, I got married. I bought everything, rent the apartment, just everything in one month. And now my wife, she is pregnant, and she is two months and six days. And we think—we are not sure—we think it is a boy. It is up to God, but we think it is a boy, because of the way he sleeps. We have some picture of him. It's exciting.

"My dad, when I called him, he started crying and gave the phone to my mom and she started crying and gave the phone to my sister and she started crying. They are happy for me and they are sad that they missed that time—they are supposed to be with me. And also, when we married, they talked with me on the Internet after the party was done. We opened the Internet and just wait, stayed all dressed, and they saw us. They make their own party; they start singing for us. It was on Yahoo messenger. They talked to us for one or two hours. After that they let us go. Yeah. It's a good experience here. My dad, he is very proud on me. He said, 'When you said I am going to United States, I trust you to go there and I don't care what people say, but I am very proud of you. You are going to be equipped for it.' And stuff like that. And now he thinks that since I am married, I am good."

To close his story, Senan starts speaking about refugees in general, and the challenges they face while trying to make a new home here.

"Refugees...okay, I am working here, and almost know most of the things, but if you go to your own life as a refugee outside, many things you don't know how to do. I am still not registered for my marriage. I don't know where to go, what I am supposed to do. I try to use the Internet, and there is a lot of information and you have to do this and that, and I don't know what to do. Because the Imam is licensed by the city. It's too many things confusing like that.

"Credit—like if you open a credit card in a bank and the first time, until now, you don't know how to use it, probably. How to get scores for your credit, how to buy your house, how to build your credit. Many things are difficult for refugees. I don't know how to ride the bus right now. I should go to NAREW[62] class. One time I rode the bus with a friend and 'til now I don't know how to ride the bus. I just use my car. One time in the United States I just rode one time, for a small distance, like five minutes. It's too many things are difficult.

"When you are a refugee, you come here with all this package of information, you have to do that—you have to go to the county to apply for food support. You don't know where food support is, or where cash

---

62. NAREW is MCC Refugee Service's cultural orientation class for new arrivals. Students in the class meet a representative from Metro Transit and learn to ride the bus on the first day of the class.

support is. You don't know what RCA is. It's Refugee Cash Assistance, but you don't know what it is. You don't know how to use your EBT card. How do you know there is money in your EBT card?

"Sometimes you are Arabic and they bring you an interpreter who is Somali but is speaking Arabic, and he is translating through the interviews and you can't understand anything because it's not the real Arabic. You are not getting the information you need to get. It is so confusing.

"It's not easy for refugees. I still am not really good at English. But you have the words to communicate with each other and to do your job. But many things, many words, you cannot just describe things like you would in your own language. If you are talking to somebody about a bank or a credit card, you don't have the words you need for that context. This is not your own language."

Even though life is difficult at times, Senan has many hopes for the future and is proud to live in the United States.

"I wish—I want to apply to a bank to get a house, and not be paying the rent to the landlord, but to pay my own rent to the bank and own my own house.

"Always my wife, she asks, 'Do you think to go back to Iraq?' I said, 'I am never going to Iraq.' Believe me, I am not lying now. Every time I see a flag, I say, 'This is my flag. The other flag is not my flag.' She says, 'Why?' I tell her, 'The country that don't need you there, that is not my country. The country that brought me and said, 'This is your life, you can live here and do anything you want in here'—that is my country. Not the country that kicked you out."

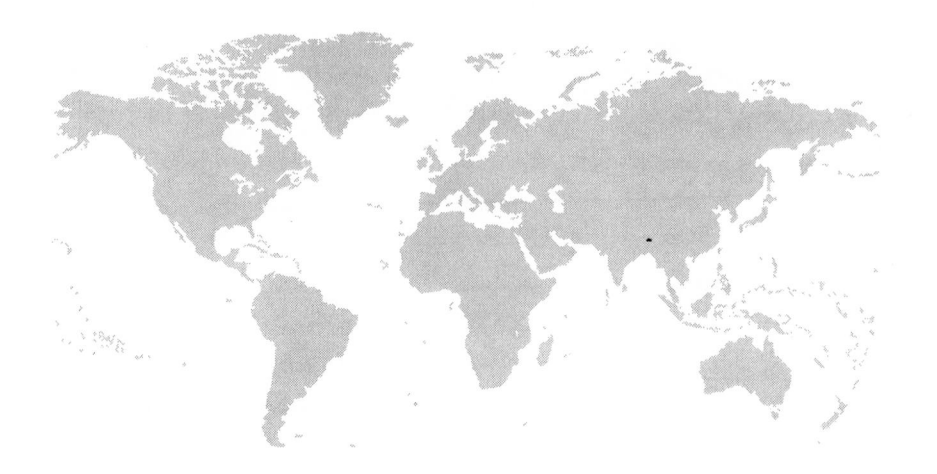

Bhutan

Over the past two years, 202 Bhutanese refugees have resettled in Minnesota.[63] Although their ancestors are originally from Nepal, this group lived and farmed in southern Bhutan, retaining its original Nepali language and Hindu religion. In Bhutan, this ethnic group was known as the Lhotsampas, and its growing numbers caused worry among the majority Druk ethnic group, indigenous northern Bhutanese people who speak Dzongkha and practice Buddhism.

Fear of the Lhotsampas demanding more power in government caused the Druks to pass a series of harsh laws during the 1980s aimed at curbing this possibility. The laws, known as Bhutanization, imposed Druk religion, culture, and language while banning what the Lhotsampas had retained of their Nepali heritage. The laws also disenfranchised and revoked citizenship for nearly all Lhotsampas, and the Lhotsampas began to flee.

After temporary relief was provided in India, the Lhotsampas moved to refugee camps in Nepal.[64] Both Bhutan and Nepal are nestled between

63. Minnesota Department of Health, "Primary Refugee Arrivals to Minnesota."
64. Center for Applied Linguistics, "Bhutanese Refugees in Nepal."

India and China, and both have similar mountainous geography and tropical climates.[65] The UNHCR reports that over eighty-nine thousand refugees still live in Nepal's refugee camps. [66]

The following three stories come from four members of the same family. They tell their family's story from unique perspectives and they illustrate how, even when a family has the same refugee journey, the impact of the experience on their memories is as varied as the people themselves.

---

65. CIA World Factbook, "Bhutan."

66. UNHCR.org, "Bhutan."

Krishna:
Father, Future US Citizen

Krishna is a Bhutanese refugee who now calls Minnesota home. He tells his story through the interpretation of his younger son, Shailesh. Krishna has not yet learned English in his six months in the United States, but always finds nonverbal ways to communicate successfully, and is eager to share his story. Krishna's story unfolds in the chill of his Minneapolis apartment. The apartment is cold because the windows aren't sealed and the cost of electric heat is so high.

Like the majority of the Bhutanese refugees coming to the US, Krishna grew up in southern Bhutan. His family members were farmers who grew crops typical for the region: "Rice, wheat, and all the crops," Shailesh translates. "Also I had a cow, many cows. The cows slept at home. Cows, buffalo, sheep, goat, and chicken.

"All the family went out to the field to work. In Bhutan, if a child is about five years old, they start work in the field. My parents told us to do that work, to harvest grass for the cows. Sometimes they told me to take the cow to the forest. When I was in Bhutan, I saw that all people do the same work, so I did not feel difficulty."

Krishna's mother was his father's first wife. After having two sons with Krishna's mother, his father married again. Krishna explains what happened next. "My father separated from me and my mom. We sit near the jungle, with nobody near our house. They quarreled with each other. My mother could not live with my father, because when I was small, my father beat her too much. She left and married another. I only saw her once after that, thirty-six years later." Krishna was only five or six when his mother left and he went to live with his grandparents. When Krishna's father remarried, Krishna and his brother rejoined the family.

At eighteen, while still living with his father, Krishna met his wife. "I myself married with Nar Maya—my father cannot do anything." Krishna's father was upset, but his wife's parents were happy with the marriage.

"When I was twenty-one, I am grown up. I was going to the field to do my work when my stepbrother and stepsister told something bad about me to my father and stepmother. After I returned from the work, they beat me, said I am bad. I left home. They were telling lies. It's not the culture [to beat], but they did."

This was not new; Krishna had suffered abuse at the hands of his father and stepmother throughout his childhood. In fact, he still suffers from the results of these beatings. "Still I have pain and I am not able to sit like [cross-legged], so I sit like this." Krishna crouches on the floor, his ankles and bare feet sticking out of his cotton pants.

Through Shailesh, Krishna tells that happened when he left. "I did not say anything to my parents, I just left. After leaving, I did not eat anything for three days. I just drank water. This was in a mountainous area." After three days he came across a house. "I had no money. I asked them [for] drinking water and I drank the water. Then I wanted to travel with by bus, but I had no money. I walked and walked and it was very dark. After maybe forty kilometers, I saw a house. It is dark and I stayed in that house for the night, but the people in that house say not to sit here, because my father will come to the house and act badly to us—you should go from here.

"After that, there is an Indian house where I sit one month and fifteen days. The owner of the house is a businessman and I told him all about me. I had to work in his shop selling goods to the customer like rice, fruit, and biscuit...apple, oranges...mango.

"After one month in the Indian people's house, [the Indian man] took me to my mother's brother's son. I sit there another nine, ten years. They have a large family and are also very rich. He did business work, like a Cub Food business. The cousin had three [children], one son and two daughters. But they are now in Nepal. Now he buy the house and land and sells to another."

Nar Maya, Krishna's wife, did not know where he had gone when he left his father's home.

"When I left the house—my parents' house—my wife was pregnant." At first Nar Maya did not live with Krishna's father, but after their daughter was born, he came for her. "He [Krishna's father] took Nar Maya to his house to do the work. He treated her badly. They were so bad to her and also my brother. But after three years, I came to her and said 'I will work and make money and I will come back, and I will take you.'"

Krishna worked in his cousin's field, and when his daughter was three, he came for his wife and child. "When they were in my parents' house, their clothes are not good; they were not provided for. I take them to my cousin's brother's house and they provided clothes to them." Prakash, Krishna's second child, was born during this time. "I worked and when I owned some money, I bought land for us. After that, Shailesh is born. I buy myself land and I work for myself."

Four years later, things changed for the family. "There was a big rally in Bhutan. In Bhutan there are no human rights [for the Lhotshampa[67] people]. They asked for the human rights. The government sent military to all the houses. They came in the nighttime and the daytime and they beat the people. They killed like that.

"After the rally, I lived there for two years. In daytime, we worked in the field; at the nighttime, the military came and captured Lhotshampas, took them and beat them. So at night, we went to the forest to sleep. There is too much rain in Bhutan and we sit in the [forest] in the raining time also. It was very difficult.

"One time, they captured me. When they came to the house, I say that I have not done anything and they leave, but another group came. They

---

67. *Lhotshampa* means "southerner" in Dzongkha, the national language of Bhutan. The term refers to the ethnic Nepali people in Bhutan.

do not ask questions. Many other people they shoot and they killed. I was not. They left me in the middle of the way.

"Sometimes when the Bhutan military—army—attack, they cut off one leg. Sometimes they cut off the hand and they throw it to the truck. Many people are dying in Bhutan. So difficult. Sometimes the military take the husband and wife and they tie them. They take the wife to this side, the husband to that side, and they do whatever they can to the wife in front of the husband. The parents and the children, they see from the house.

"We moved at night. Januka was six, Prakash was four, Shailesh was two, and Renuka was one and a half years old. We did not take anything from our house when we moved, because I carried Prakash and held hands with Januka. Nar Maya carried Shailesh and Renuka. We walked and walked. There were two big forests, and in the forest, there is tiger, lion, elephant. The elephant are so bad in Bhutan; they kill the people."

One night while walking, Krishna heard the sounds of elephants. Suddenly, the family found themselves in the middle of a herd. "They are all around us. We keep quiet and sit in the middle."

After the elephant herd moved past them, the family continued walking to India. "I had some money, but there is place called the Asum where there were men with guns. They asked for the money and I gave it to them."

After walking for hours and hours, they arrived in India where they joined other Bhutanese families, and local villagers provided the group with some food. "We sit there for five days. [Then] the Indian army came and put us in the truck. They took us and they threw us to the Bengali state. They threw us at night, at 11:00 p.m., and we didn't know any language. We didn't have any money because they had stolen it, and it is winter season, February. How can the children sleep like this in the road? And when morning time came, at 5:00 a.m., again the Bengali police came. They took us to the Nepal border and at 9:00 p.m. they threw us to Nepal.

"There is a long bridge [between] India and Nepal. After we crossed, the Nepal police captured us and asked, 'Where you are coming from? Why are you coming?' They all ask that. We have not eaten anything and we all are crying because of our hunger. The Nepal police made a statement and took us to another truck. It is midnight."

The Nepali police brought them to a temporary camp called Mai. "There was one small house [for everyone] and there was nobody to cook the food. There was not any food to cook. We had no pots to cook. We sit like this that night. It was very cold and the wind blew all night. We sat very quietly there and we cut the night like that.

"There were no tents. They are not prepared. Before we came, there [were already] some Bhutanese from Bhutan. In the morning they asked, 'You have already eat the food?' And we said 'No, we have not.' They provided some of the food, like rice. At the time when they gave the rice, we had no matches to go in the fire, and no pot. They gave us the pot to cook and we cooked the food, returned that pot.

"After some days, the Red Cross provided food and some tents. We lived in small tent. It was very difficult to live. The wind blew and the fire would go out. We spent six months in the Mai camp. Many people there died. Too much cholera.

"Januka and Prakash were sick. On one day, thirty-five, forty-five people might die. In front of our house there were twenty-two people in one family—after, there were only seven people. I don't know whether the seven people died or not; we moved before then. We went to the Goldhap Camp.

"When we moved the UNHCR[68] provided us with some food. They saw that we are refugees and countries like the United States, Canada—they helped the refugees. They gave a little food for the family and I worked outside the camp. I worked in things like house construction, road construction, and business. Also [as a] school security guard, and with Save the Children as a volunteer. I added to my house the solar plate and I put light to my house."

After fifteen years in Goldhap, Krishna was injured doing construction

---

68. UNHCR refers to the Office of the United Nations High Commissioner for Refugees, also called the UN Refugee Agency.

work. "Fifty kilogram iron fell on my foot." Then he suffered another, more serious accident. "Wood fell from the second floor. It is come and hit me in the back and also to the leg. My back was broken. They referred me to a doctor outside the refugee camp. I was at home for eight months. All the blood...sometimes if I had pain, I saw the doctor."

After this, and at the time of a fire that spread across the camp, Krishna could not return to work. "When the fire happened, I was in the house. I would walk, but when I walked a long distance, I was pained. When I stood, I also was pained, and when I sit like that, I was pained. I had many medicines, but they were not sufficient."

The fire in the camp happened just before the family came to the United States. Krishna lost all of the family's possessions and money. "All were gone from the fire. When I came from Bhutan to Minnesota, I did not bring anything, because all was gone by the fire. After the fire, we lived in the forest for a full month. The different organizations, they helped us, and after four months, we came to the United States.

"I thought very badly in that time, because I missed my neighbors and relatives, but here it is good. I like the United States. The process for us to come took six months. When we came, we are MCC clients. All the things they provide, they are from the MCC. I give thanks to the MCC and also the people of the United States.

"We came with only one bag each, with some clothes. MCC helped by making appointments to the hospital and they gave materials, too. In all things they are helping us, each and everything. After the fire happened in the camp, we were in the forest for a month, so when we came to the United States, I was very happy to sit in a house."

Now Krishna and his family are living in North Minneapolis. "After winter, we will change to another house. It is so expensive and sometimes Januka and Prakash have only three or four days of work a week. This week, they have done only three days. It is difficult to pay the rent, water and electricity, gas, and travel loans.[69]"

---

69. Refugees' plane tickets to come to the United States are given with the understanding that recipients will pay back the cost of travel expenses through a loan program.

But Krishna has hopes for the future. "I will become a citizen of the United States, and grow old in the United States, and die in the United States. If I am well, I will work. When I was in Nepal, I used to work, but because I am not well, it is difficult. I hope that I will buy a house and a car, be a citizen, and sit in the United States."

Krishna says he does not worry about himself or his children losing touch with their Bhutanese culture. "I do not feel bad," he says through Shailesh. "I want to learn the American culture. My mentor, he took me to see the Christmas lights. I am happy. I feel okay. All the people who live in the world, American or Nepali, we all are equal, the same."

Prakash & Shailesh:
Brothers, Thankful Survivors

On a late December afternoon, two Bhutanese brothers tell the story of their journey from Bhutan to the United States. Prakash and Shailesh are Krishna's sons, and they now tell their version of their family's story.

Prakash, the older of the brothers, begins. "We lived in the southern part of Bhutan, the district of Sarpang. My parents were farmers. Just our family lived together. We live in Nepali community." The Lhotshampa have Nepali heritage and speak the Nepali language.

Prakash does not remember much of Bhutan, saying, "It was a dream for me." He left when he was only four or five. Shailesh says, "I also think the same. It is like a dream."

Prakash does remember leaving the country. "It was midnight. My mom and dad, they wake me up from the bed. 'Let's move, let's move,' they said, and before we wake up, they already taken some stuff [to the forest]. They take us towards the forest, and we come to the India by walking. They said we have to go to another country. We should not have to leave; we were very small. We don't know why we have to move, and I don't ask anything.

"I follow them, my parents. I remember not that much, but we cross the forest and after that, we reach to India. India we live in for one day, and after that there was some army from India."

"Bengal," Shailesh clarifies quietly.

"They take us to Bengal State," Prakash continues. "And the Bengal army, they take all of us to Nepal. My family and other families. They put all of the people in the truck and they take us to the border of Nepal and India and they thrown there." He snorts. "We had no house and we live there for two days—five days. At night we live in the street."

Shailesh only remembers this a little. His cell phone starts ringing, a mellow whistling tone, but he ignores it and keeps talking. "After that the Nepalese police, they come and talk about 'Who are you?' They take our family and other families to the Mai Camp and we sit there three or four months, I think. After that, we sit in a refugee camp, the Goldhap Camp."

Prakash adds, "The Nepal police used to come [to Mai Camp] and say, 'It's not allowed to make a house here; you move,' and they thrown all our tent and we had to make them again. Again they say, 'This is not the area; this is the forest area. It's not allowed to make a tent here.' Again, again they thrown from there. And later on, the UNHCR know that there are refugees from Bhutan going back to Nepal, and they manage for resettlement. We live in Mai Camp and they provide some rice for the food, but not for sufficient, just a little. That was on the bank of the river. There was no work, no work."

Prakash explains that they lived in temporary shelter: "Tents, because it was so new. We lived closer to each other." The brothers, their two sisters, and their parents shared one tent. "After that there is some...epi— what is that, there is one kind of disease—that come in the refugee camp—and many people used to die."

"Cholera, yeah," Shailesh says, and Prakash elaborates. "Due to the pollution and all. There is a lot of pollution. Me and my mom became sick there, when we sit there."

But they survived. "Yeah. That is good work." They both laugh.

"At night when we sleep, the bed used to shake," Prakash adds. "We wake up at the night and we used to ask our dad, 'What is happening?'"

Prakash and his brother say that it felt like an earthquake, but the shaking did not come from under the earth—it was the vibrations of a machine burying people.

Prakash continues, "Then we move to different camp. We lived in Goldhap. First they give us tent same as Mai, only the tent that we put the plastic over. But later on we make a wall of bamboo. And it was quite good.

"They give the rice, refined oil, and kerosene for lamp," Prakash continues. "There is no electricity there, so we have to make lamp with kerosene. And they provide some vegetables." Shailesh's phone starts ringing again, and Prakash talks over it. "Cabbage, chili, and all. Not much. And later on there is a school." Shailesh's phone beeps with a voicemail.

"When we come from Mai to the Goldhap camp, there is not any school," Prakash goes on. "They teach at the forest site. I was so small at that time. After one year, they construct the school. Blooming Lotus English School. They teach one subject as Nepali, and one subject that is Dzongkha. It is Bhutan language. Others are in English."

"I think student life is the better one," Prakash says. "I have got many friends in the school. And when I came here, I miss them a lot. Some friends are already in US, now but in different state."

"Also in different country," Shailesh adds.

During their free time in the camp, they used to play sports. Prakash remembers. "And Shailesh is intelligent in football. And we used to play table tennis, volleyball, cricket, basketball. They manage for running competition. They provide the prize; they give us sometimes... seal. You know seal?"

"Yeah, yeah; they provide medal. And some they provide with soap and very funny picture." Prakash laughs. "And sometimes there is the competition from camp to camp... and our Goldhap is the most senior one."

In addition to playing sports, they played house: their little sister Renuka made them. "Still here she is playing," Prakash laughs. "We have our three-year-old cousin with her, so she still plays."

The school in Goldhap was free through level ten and beyond costed money, but Caritas[70] provided help. "After we complete the eleven and twelve, all the money we have to pay by ourself," Prakash says. "Inside the camp, there is no job. For job we have to go out of the camp and search." Some farmed, while others worked in construction. They ended up working in a small shop where they sold goods from the camp.

---

70. Caritas Nepal is a nongovernmental organization which works among the underprivileged in issues involving human rights abuses by empowering them toward self-sufficiency in their communities.

Just before the family left Goldhap, there was a fire in the camp. "It started from one house," Prakash says. "Later on, we came to know that it was the fire from the gas. Cylinder gas.

"At that time, we are at home, talking with family and neighbor. And there is some quarrel we heard. We move towards the quarrel site and we see—there is a fire! And we start to fight with the fire. It comes greater and greater. We throw water and green leaves, but we don't [have] success. They call the firefighting, and firefighting came there after half an hour. They don't success to fight with the fire. Later on it comes to our house, and I take the materials, some foods, rice, and our clothes. The whole camp is damaged."

Shailesh wasn't at home when the fire started. "I and my friend, we are going to the market. I saw from there and it is come bright and we ran from that shop to the fire guard. We two are go for the firefighting. It's become very, very more fire. I thinks now I will go to my house to take out materials, but the fire block me and I am not success.

"Within two and half hours, it finish. All 1,328 huts had burned. I don't know where [my family] are gone and I feel very sad and I am separated from them. After fire, I search—search my family, but it is very dark, maybe it is 1:30 at night and I search and I—I do not find them. My family thought that 'He is already burn; he is not here.'

"When I search, I found one of the friend and I asked him, 'Can you know my family? Where is my family?' and he said that 'Maybe they are in the forest.' I am searching all the family and after that I think is maybe 4:00 a.m., morning. And after that I see that there is not any materials at all in our house."

"He comes at the morning," Prakash says.

There were crowds of people trying to find their family members. Finally, someone brought a microphone and people started announcing the names of those separated from their families; Shailesh was finally reunited with his.

"We live in the forest for two days," Prakash says. "After that, we live in the school. My father used to work in the school as security guard; he occupied one room, so we go there. We are not sleeping in a bed; we sleep on a floor. Only after four months did I sleep in a bed, when I come to the United States. Some people lives inside the school and people who are not, they live in the forest. They don't have any tent [at first] but after fifteen days the UNICEF provided some tents to people."

After two months, Prakash went ahead of the family to Minnesota. Shailesh says, "We already, before the fire, have started a process of resettlement to the US." Prakash says he wasn't scared, but it was difficult. "I missed all of my family and the friends. [My family] worried about how is the US. How they treat us. They may discourage us or they may do something for us."

"Yeah," Shailesh agrees. "When I come here, it is vast different from I thinks."

"We see the movies and pictures," Prakash tells me. The refugees from Goldhap would visit a nearby city with a movie theater. "And news, they said about the US and George W. Bush. He did this something in the US; he change something. Yeah. And at that time, we imagine that the US has a lot of big, big building, very tall. And when I arrive here, I found only the downtown is like that—all the homes are made up of wood and—it is different, but [some things are the] same as I thought.

"When I arrive here, I live in St. Paul. There was two guys from Nepal and I live with them for one month. [Then] I came to the church house—Mayflower Church house—before my family arrive. I manage some materials and some food for them."

Shailesh says the family did worry about Prakash before they joined him, but they were able to talk on the phone. "He told good things about the US. He said 'Come. Come fast. It's good.'"

When the family arrived, Josiah—their caseworker from MCC—and their US tie[71] met them at the airport. Prakash says, "I find the people, the employee, and all the MCC members very friendly and cooperative one and helpful one, so I want to give a lot of thanks to the MCC." The brothers' parents went on a government assistance program, as did Prakash;

---

71. "US tie" is a resettlement term referring to the family member a refugee is joining in the United States."

Januka and Shailesh enrolled in an employment program; and Renuka started attending high school. Because their parents couldn't work, the boys felt a lot of pressure, along with Januka, to start jobs as soon as possible.

Prakash got a job at a hotel, and during the Republican National Convention, Januka and Shailesh were hired as well. Shailesh only worked for twelve days. "In laundry. They don't say before 'We hire you for temporary.' But one lady, I don't know her name, she said that 'From today, you have to leave your job and search for another job and go.' And I said 'Why? I am not make any mistake,' and she said 'You are not do any mistake, but you have to leave now.'"

"She said one thing in interview—" Prakash starts.

"—and doing another," Shailesh finishes. They are clearly frustrated.

"And at the times of the interviews, she said you are provided with free lunch and all, but later on, there was no free lunch." Prakash leans back. "I take the lunch break, but my sister Januka, she doesn't take because she works a little slow.

"It is difficult. The supervisor—I don't think he is as good as I think. When I was given the training, they said that we have to work only for housekeeping, but later when I finish, they send me to do another job. Like sweeping of floor.

"And I think the supervisor make us to do more work [than the others]. He don't say others employed to do this thing, this thing, [and] this thing. But he says, me and Januka do this thing. So we don't finish in time. And they complain that [we are] late." Sonja, their job counselor, spoke with the supervisor, but Prakash and Januka still work under difficult conditions.

"Still I am working there, but I am trying to find another job. Due to the chemical we use there—" he holds out his hands; the skin is cracked and red. "I use lotion every day. I don't know what happens; it was bleeding…it was not only the hand; it was all over the body." They wear gloves, but Prakash says it doesn't help. "It is not good, so I am trying for another job."

The brothers say it has also been difficult explaining where they are from. "Some people they say, 'Are you Indian?'" Shailesh says. "And I answer that 'I am Bhutanese.' But my nationality is Nepali."

"They don't know when I say Nepal, Bhutan," Prakash tells us. "And I say, 'Do you know Mount Everest?'"

In the camp, they were able to celebrate religious holidays. "We miss our festivals," Prakash says. This year, they're going to try out Christmas; a new American friend has brought them a small plastic tree, ornaments, and stockings to hang. Their father's mentor has given them a Christmas wreath, and they made holiday cookies.

While still living in the Mayflower House, Prakash tells about a time he was outside the house, phoning Nepal. "I am walking, not three minute away from home. And I heard the 'Hi.' They said 'Hi,' and I turn and said, 'Hi.' And they have their gun. They said, 'Give me your cell phone' and I look at their gun [to see] whether it is a toy or a real one. I sense that gun was real and I thought if I don't give the cell phone to them, they may shoot me. They grab the cell phone from my hand and take out wallet from my pocket. They said, 'Go on. Move, move. Move!'

"I turn towards my home and I walk a little bit. I [look] back to them to see what direction they are going. Then I run towards my home and I phone the police and I block phone, EBT card, and the bank—the bank where I have open the checking account. I block all of the things and cell phone company. After that, I call the police and the police arrive there and they are searching. But they never found.

"I thought there is no fight in the US, but also I have a fight with two guys. I come by train [home from work]. When I was in the train, I sit on the seat and they spits toward me."

"From the mouth," Shailesh clarifies.

"Yeah, from the mouth. No reason, I simply sit there. They spit toward my cheek and ear. And I turn over there and I said, 'What do you want, man?' I ask only that much. They said something—I don't know what they are saying; I don't understand. And I sit quietly and when Nicollet Mall come, I exit there. And they also exit there. And come backside and they do like this, like this"—Prakash mimes someone pushing at his shoulder from behind—"and they say something I don't

understand. I feel very very angry and I turn and I catch their clothes."
He gestures to the front of his shirt. "I gave one punch to them. They spit
towards me and again they come to fight. Two of them—I think they are
the age of me.

"I give one punch to them, the other comes to kick me, and then I
fight with the two of them but they have put pant here"—he gestures on
his legs to indicate sagged pants—"and I think that is why they have the
difficulty to kick. One boy has bleeding from the nose and he ran away
and the other comes to fight. I kick him and more people gather there.
They said, 'Run, run; they may call their friend,' and I run toward the bus.
I have to take twenty-two number bus but I take the fourteen number just
to [get away].

"I have the long hair and I thought from my hair they may recognize
me. I cut the hair. They hurt me but not as [badly as I hurt them]."

"In Nepal we used to fight. Nepal is very different from here, and
there...there is no sufficient strong rules. They have it in the law, but
people don't follow. We had fights—too many—so we are experienced in
fighting."

"There is fighting [between the people] outside the camp and camp
people," Shailesh explains.

"They came with the gang," Prakash says. "We have a lot of fight
with the—not only the hand—"

"With the gun," Shailesh helps.

"With the gun, but I won't—I haven't played with the gun," Prakash
says. "There is a lot of fight. I don't know, there is the discrimination
between—between the—"

"Refugee," Shailesh suggests.

"Refugee and the Nepalese people. We are also Nepalese, but we are
[also] Bhutanese. And there is discrimination between Bhutanese Nepalese and the Nepalese. We are not supposed to bear that discrimination."

"I love my motherland Bhutan, but our culture and our traditional
[ways] all are in Nepal. We are Nepali. When we are in Bhutan we are
not allowed to celebrate our culture. That is why we back to Nepal as
refugee," says Prakash.

"We should not say that it is done [only] by the Drukpas,"[72] Prakash tells us, "That was done by the—"

"Government," Shailesh says at the same time his brother does.

Prakash nods. "Yeah."

"After they are not allowed reading Nepali book, our people ask about the human rights. They not give any of the rights to the Bhutanese people. Some army are come in the house and they take some parent from the house. They shoot the gun and killed sometime, and they put people in the jail. So many people are killed by the government. All the people—we move to Nepal," Shailesh concludes.

"Yeah, we talk about all the things we come from—how we have come from Bhutan as a refugee. That's the reason. I don't know [if we will go back] but I think we will settle in US. For visiting, we may go there." As Prakash speaks, his brother nods in agreement.

In the future, Prakash wants to study math like he did in Nepal, where he focused on business mathematics. "I am still trying to get the GED," he says.

Shailesh says, "I also interested in studying in the United States. I think I have to get the GED, after I have to go to the college. I hope I will take the commerce and economic."

Prakash says, "I want to give more thanks to the United States and the people whoever are in the United States. I want to give thanks to the organization that help us when we are in Nepal like UNHCR, Caritas Nepal. And special thanks to the US government and the people."

Shailesh closes with this: "When we are in Nepal, we have no citizenship. We sit in Nepal seventeen years and they not give any citizenship."

Here, in the US, they are on a track to citizenship; they can apply for their green cards after a year and for citizenship in five.

Shailesh says, "I give thanks to the organization that helps the refugee, UNHCR, Caritas Nepal, Lutherans, Red Cross, and the organization that helps to resettle the refugee in the United States and the others country. I give thanks to all the people."

---

72. Those belonging to the dominant school and state religion of Bhutan; a branch of Tibetan Buddhism.

Januka:
Daughter, Witness of Change

Januka, sister of Prakash and Shailesh and the daughter of Krishna, tells her version of their family refugee story. Januka, in her early twenties, begins her story at the edges of her memory.

"Bhutan...it is just like a dream. I am so small. I just remember how they treat us sometimes. I just remember a little bit." She knows that her father bought a plot of land where the family farmed rice. This was when her first brother, Prakash, was born. "I was happy to be a big sister. Then we moved to another place, and my brother Shailesh was born there. I was five years old, and I helped my parents, cooking food and helping with the cows, oxen, and goats." She also helped take care of her younger siblings. "I fed them and watched them, and cleaned the house. My mom and my dad were busy in the field most of the day. They left early in the morning, came back to take lunch, and went out again. Sometimes when there was a moon, they would work in the moonlight." Nearby families would all help each other when it was time to harvest.

"I did not go to school, there was no chance. At the time, the Drukpa people did not allow the Lhotshampa[73] people to join the school." Januka also remembers the Drukpas coming with trucks and stealing the family's rice paddy harvest. "They took more land and kept for us only a little. And one day, when I was five or six years old, the army came to our home and searched for my father. He was working on the land, but they found

---

73. The ethnic Nepalese population of Bhutan, generally Hindu.

157

him and handcuffed him. They said they will take him to jail, and they took him away, but on the way they suddenly left him. We don't know what happened; we don't know why. The army came often to take people, and they killed some of them. Others they put in jail. They would burn houses and steal the harvest, like ours."

The army continued looking for her father, Krishna. "He hid in the jungle with some relatives. We brought them food. They spent many days like that, before we left. Then, in the early morning, we left. I was small, but I helped carry things. We walked into the jungle, even though it was dangerous—there were many elephants."

The family crossed into the Bengal state. "The people there were so kind. They gave us rooms to sleep. I don't remember how many days we stayed. Then the Indian government came with trucks and took us to Nepal. It was so troubling. The police of Nepal questioned us, and then they put us on another truck. We came to the bank of a river, and we prayed—in the Hindu religion we believe that the river has a god, and we prayed.

"Then we stayed five or six months in Mai, a temporary camp, but it was very dangerous and the conditions were bad. There was sickness. The wind never stopped, and it brought sandstorms. It kept us from making fires. We tried to cook in our tents, but they were plastic, and the storms would blow them down. We ate beaten rice.

"After five or six months, we moved to Goldhap camp. It was not good, but it was better than Mai. At least we had the chance to go to school. We lived in a bamboo hut with a thatched roof, and it had just one room for all six of us. It was so congested, and every year we had to repair the hut. After ten years, we made it wider illegally—the agency didn't allow it, but we could not manage. We made three bedrooms and one kitchen."

While in the camp, Januka was able to start school. She enjoyed it, but found some classes difficult, and it was hard to find a quiet place in the crowded camp to study. She repeated three of the classes, graduated, and started taking vocational courses offered by the Caritas Nepal NGO. "I was trained in hair styling and photography, and after that, I completed the beads and garlands training on making necklaces. I didn't finish the hair styling course because after one month, we were ready to come to the United States."

By that time, the family had been in the camp for seventeen years. During their sixteenth year, on March 1, there was a fire. "In one house, a cylinder of gas exploded. We were home, finishing dinner, and we heard a noise outside. We went to look and saw the fire. At the same time a big storm came, so it was difficult to put out the flames. The whole camp burned down. We crossed the river and ran into the forest. We stayed there for four months in tents. It was so difficult. The local people from the village came and stole things, and there was a big rainstorm. We lost everything. All our property for seventeen years was gone.

"Fifteen days before we left, they started distributing bamboo and plastic for people to begin rebuilding." Januka's family didn't rebuild because they knew they were coming to the US; they had sent her brother Prakash ahead and were excited to follow. Januka says, "We were not worried about him because our cousin was here. And before we followed him, I thought the US has only big, big houses. I thought it was like down-town Minneapolis. Not just me, all the people thought that."

Januka wanted to join English classes as soon as she came, but instead she had to start working a rotating schedule that didn't allow for regular courses. She tells of other difficulties, too: not knowing the bus route to visit her uncle, not speaking English fluently, and the economy—if not for the recession, Januka and her brothers might have found other jobs, but as it is, they have decided to stay where they are for the moment.

But in spite of these troubles, Januka has enjoyed her new life and describes what she's liked best: "Visiting different places, like the museums and the Hindu temple, and watching movies. I liked celebrating Thanksgiving, and Christmas." Even though her family is Hindu, they've decided to try out American holidays. And they've started watching television: the WWF smack down every Friday, and *Superstars of Dance*. They like court shows. She adds, "[And] crime shows, police chases. We learn from there what we have to do or not do, how the police know things—in their police car there is a computer, and everywhere they keep cameras."

Meanwhile, Januka has noticed how vastly different the gender roles are in the US. "In our country, there is no chance for women to do higher jobs. Women drive buses here, but in Nepal only men drive the bus. In the towns, maybe a couple of women drive a car or motorcycle. Here there are women everywhere: in the offices, in the hospital, everywhere. In Bhutan women usually work on the land and in the home; they cook food and take care of the children. They don't get a chance to do other work. Here in the US, there is more freedom. Women can become anything: a doctor, a nurse, anything."

In the coming years, Januka plans to continue living with her family. "I don't think about marriage because my parents don't have jobs. We are working to support our family. I am close to my parents and brothers and sister. But if my parents get jobs and somebody asks for my hand and I like to marry, then maybe I will marry. It is difficult to marry here, I think. I would like to marry in my community, because our culture would be the same."

One worry that Januka shares with her parents is about practicing their death rites in the US. "According to our culture, when somebody dies, we burn the body. We stay without clothes, sleep on the floor, and fast—we take food only once a day—for thirteen days. We make a fire, and a special person reads a holy book. When my father's mother died, we did not have to do all of this because she left her first husband and went to another, but otherwise we have to do it everyday for thirteen days. That is difficult here; we don't get the time off from our jobs.

"One of our relatives died here. In our culture, the son gives fire to the body of his parent, but here the son flipped a switch—we heard it was a remote thing. My parents are afraid. They don't know how this works here. And we heard that they had to pay five thousand dollars for the cremation.

"Life is expensive here," Januka says. "It is good—yeah, many things are good, but some of the things...it is difficult for us. After a while, I hope, we will adapt."

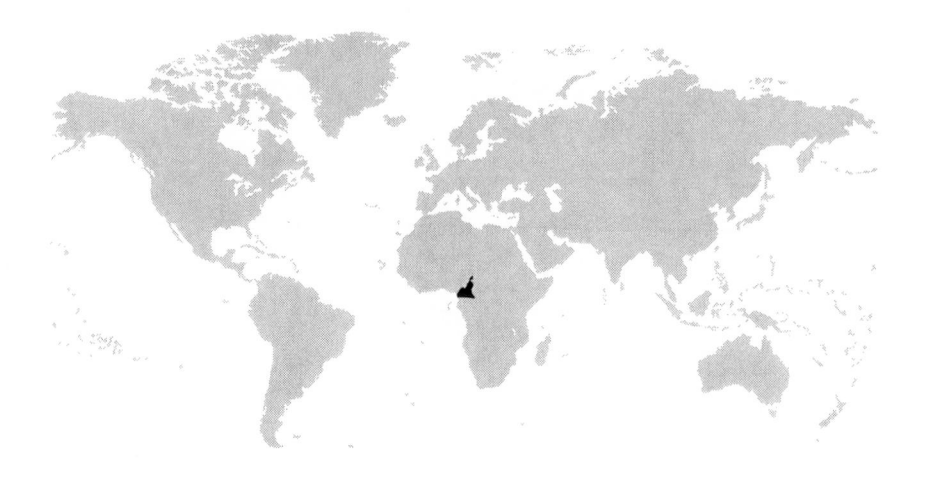

Cameroon

Many of today's tensions in Cameroon, from which over seventeen thousand refugees have fled, originate in its colonial legacy. The French controlled part of present-day Cameroon, while the British controlled the rest, and as a result, English and French emerged as two competing languages when a unified Cameroon gained independence in 1961.[74][75]

Cameroon, located just below Nigeria on Africa's west coast, also hosts refugees from Chad and the Central African Republic. Many fleeing Cameroonians sought refuge in Nigeria. By 2009, 177 Cameroonian refugees have resettled in Minnesota.[76]

Cameroon has a tropical climate along its mountainous Atlantic coast, while it tends to be semiarid and hot in the north. The majority of the population speaks either English or French, although many people speak numerous indigenous languages. Similarly, while many Cameroonians practice either Christianity or Islam, many others honor indigenous religions.[77]

74. UNHCR.org, "Cameroon."

75. Emily Brady, "A Year of Living Nervously." *The New York Times* online.

76. MN Department of Health, "Primary Refugee Arrivals to Minnesota."

77. CIA World FactBook, "Cameroon."

Bayongson:
Civil Servant, Man of God

Bayongson tells his story in a meeting room at the MCC office, sitting at one of the long, rectangular tables grouped in a square under the buzzing florescent lights. Bayongson wears light gray slacks, a purple sweater over a crisp collared shirt, and a traditional Cameroonian hat. He is fifty-four years old and carries himself with the authoritative air of a dignified elder.

He sits down, crosses his ankles, and folds his hands on the table before him. "I am Bayongson, the son of an African father Casina Bayong and my mother, Anastasia Akwen," he introduces himself. "They are of late memory. I am the youngest child, the only male in a family with five daughters. I was born in West Cameroon, [which is] different from East Cameroon. West Cameroon is English, British. I was educated with a British education, and I did all my primary, secondary, high school, university—all in the English Saxon tradition. But East Cameroon is guided by the French culture.

"West Cameroon was an independent entity until 1961, when we had a historic merger with East Cameroon. But this historic merger, this marriage, was not consummated; it was abrogated by the East Cameroonians reverting to the idea of one united Cameroon, going back to La République, which was the original name of the East Cameroonians. We, the West Cameroonians, said we did not want this; we came for a marriage of unity. Our unity was to be two independent states in one union, not that one state is assimilated by the other. They gradually assimilated us as though we were a conquered race. That has been hidden; they do not include it into the educational history in Cameroon, so that the children do not know now. Their reason is for greater assimilation, but we who are the elderly want to maintain that history and pass it to our children.

"So now we are fighting for our independence, for the sovereignty of West Cameroon. La République, the East Cameroonian French, want to eliminate us. When we say we don't want this union, they send the army and police to harass and arrest us for trying to venture out, to disclose our identities as West Cameroonians, to let our children know how we came to be like this. We are called secessionists, but we are not secessionists. The real political analysis of secession is to have an integral part leave. We are not an integral part; we were two persons who came together, and it is just like the contract of marriage, a unity, and when that unity is not in the future consummated, what do you do? Divorce.

"So that is how it is. Now we are protesting to the United Nations through the West Cameroonian movement. We have so many movements that fight for this sovereign state. Some people identify themselves as from the Southern Cameroonian National Council, and it is one and the same thing, West Cameroonian, too. If somebody tells you South Cameroonian Council and West Cameroonian, they are the same thing.

"We are targeted now to be eliminated. That is why you see those escaping to come here to the US. Before I came...if I tell you exactly how I came here, it is really so humanely debasing. I was arrested. Tortured.

"My job was as a town planning administrator. I worked for more than thirty-two years in the civil service, under the government as a civil servant. Before we went into this merger, I had been in the West Cameroonian government as a town administrator for around five years. When we did the merger, the civil service merged. I worked for twenty-seven years in La République.

"Though I was in the government, I was also a politician. I was preaching a democratic rule. The present regime of Biya[78] is not democratic. There is no democracy in Cameroon—not an ounce of democracy.

---

78. Paul Biya, the current president and chairman of the Cameroon People's Democratic Movement party.

It is totally totalitarian, a civilian military rule. They take the civilian and out him like a puppet. The real power is the military.

"When I was there, you would be arrested, dumped in the prison, in the cells—I had been to the cell more than forty-two times, can you imagine? Not for any crime—no civil service or embezzlement crime—only because I was agitating for democracy and the sovereignty of southern Cameroon.

"Sometimes I was held for a night, sometimes for a week. Sometimes I was interrogated and released after a week or two weeks. I have never been there for more than a month. In our grassroots movement, I was the district treasurer,[79] and when you want to organize a protest in your district, you must have someone to lead the protest; we, the executives, must lead the protest. So when they arrest, you are arrested.

"So they targeted me, and my family could not put their heads out in society from fear of being killed. It hampered my children's education. Going to school, they feared identifying themselves as my children."

Bayongson explains how his political philosophy developed and how he became a politician in the first place. "I grew up with the philosophy of reading, going to school," he says. "My parents were illiterate peasant farmers, doing subsistence farming, but my father had ventured and did a bit of trading. He tread on foot to neighboring countries and bought and sold articles, so they could use that to educate me.

"I stayed at home until my university, where people were trying to assimilate us by forcing us to do studies only in French. I did not know French, so I could not be prepared. I tried; I did what I could to a point, but then I could not bear it and I had to leave. We who had the Anglo-Saxon education could not have the chance of an equal education.

At this point Bayongson explains how he met his current wife, Comfort, and started a family. "My parents were always itchy that I should marry to a girl from my village," he says, "because I first had a marriage which was not successful with a woman who was not from my village—we did not speak the same dialect. I think that brought us some problems.

---

79. Bamenda Electoral District of Social Democratic Force (SDF), North West Province.

I don't know, maybe other matrimonial problems emanated, and when that happened, the marriage could not be consummative. My parents now told me that once bitten, twice shy. After that unsuccessful marriage with a nonnative, now I must be very careful not to repeat that, so then I thought that I should be married to my own.

"Comfort and myself come from the same village. I cannot say exactly how we met; I think she knows better—that memory is faint in me.

"Our love grew until the aspect of marriage entered. When we got married, I think in 1984; Comfort was around twenty-two years old. I was still working, and she did her education and then stopped. She now became a housewife. When she came, she was quite fruitful, so she stayed up to a month and she was with child. Comfort has four children, all boys, in three deliveries. The twins are the last two.

"In my tradition, twins are looked on as supernatural; we have the belief that they are not normal. When you deliver twins, you do what they call eye cleansing. You rejoice differently; you do certain traditions and make a certain special shrine for them. You make a certain calabash, which is only used for them, and use leaves that can only be used by a mother who has delivered twins.

"The twins really are abnormal, I am telling you, though you may doubt it. Their behavior is not normal like the behavior of single children. Sometimes they have astray behavior. They communicate in the astray world with each other and with other twins. They do their extra communication. I had never believed it until my own twins came.

"The father of a twin is respected, and when the mother of a twin comes to a place, she is given extra honor. She is just a superwoman, a woman who has brought abnormal children. So they give you respect. The parents have a title: my title is *tangi*, and it means father of abnormal children—which means twins. My wife is called *mangi*."

Bayongson was involved in politics during his first marriage and continued during his second. "Even before Comfort got married to me, I was detained in jail. I was active as a politician, and even when she was pregnant with the children, I was detained, even with my first children I was detained. It was a continuous incident. My children, whenever they see a uniformed officer approaching, they would be running because they knew it was to arrest their father.

"I knew that what I was doing was for the interest of my country, for the West Cameroonians. I was fighting for their sovereignty, their liberation, their emancipation. I who really knows what happened, I must show that light to the young ones, who have only read or heard. It's me who really grew up in the system. I am a different entity, and if I don't identify myself, whom do I expect to identify?

"Even as I am here in Minnesota, I am still pushing. We marched up to the capital last year in 2007. Our chairman and myself, we presented speeches, and we were interviewed by journalists. We are not secessionists. We have not stopped. I am not going to relent, we are not going to relent until our sovereignty is achieved. Our issue is on the floor at the United Nations. It's only that the Francophone government is using corrupt means—you know the Old World human beings, so money minded they are. The officers are corrupt; they don't see our issue like a genuine issue."

Now Bayongson tells of his escape from Cameroon. "It reached a time when the search for me was just to eliminate me," he begins. "They had tortured me and discovered that I could not give up. They said to me, 'If you don't advocate for West Cameroon, everything will be good.' I told them that is over my corpse. So many times they told me, 'You will be made somebody; you will be an important person in society. You are knowledgeable, educated—look how you are wasting your education.' I told them no.

"Finally they saw that I was not bendable. So the only alternative was to eliminate me. And when I was arrested next, I was in West Cameroon and transferred to East Cameroon, to a place called Kondengui. When you are transferred there, your family members know that if you are not fortunate, that's it for you. But they cannot open their mouths to ask whether you are still there, for fear of their own being eliminated.

"I was arrested along with most of the friends I had been with. We sat in a room like this, about fifty people. They would come and call out names, five names in a night. Those people go, and the following morning you discover that you are only forty-two in the room. You cannot ask where the other people are. You don't know where they have gone or whether they are alive. They just keep taking them out and they are gone, just like that.

"When I was in university, I belonged to debate club, and one of my Francophone friends from the club went to the army and became a general in East Cameroon. I think he saw my name, or maybe he saw me moving around in this detention camp. One evening, he sent his subordinate to come and call me.

"I had in my mind that those were my last names, just saying, 'Well, once dead, that is a better way of living.' When you die, that is a better way of living. So when the subordinate came and called me, I came. When I sat down with the general, who had a knife and an arm, he asked why I was there. I said, 'I am here because of my political philosophy.' I told him I am a Western Cameroonian and I don't belong in this dictatorship regime.

"He asked if I remembered being at the university and I said yes. He asked if I remembered being very active in the debate club, and I said yes. He was not talking in French, but in a type of English that I could understand. I did not remember him at first, and then I thought, *This could be the boy who was there*... I ask if he was there with me that year.

"He said yes. Then he said that [that] was not what he has called me here for. He has called me here for this: 'You only have one option now, not two. You move to an unknown.' He said he was going to aid me and if I was successful, good; but if I was not, that was the end of my luck. He told me that all he can do is assist me. When he talked to me it was 2:00 a.m. in the morning; it was the night.

"I only had on slippers, so he gave me canvas shoes and some money, which was in the equivalent of around one hundred dollars. He asked me if I knew my way from there, and when I said no, he aided me—an assistant and himself, they drove me out. It looked like he was taking me to eliminate me because the generals and the big people had that power to eliminate.

"I think he had just felt our relationship...felt that this is a person and it is not his fault...at least that is what I was thinking.

"I know the geography of my country with my knowledge of town planning. They had seized my papers. I had no identity. I hid myself somewhere, and then the following morning, I got a vehicle to the neighboring village. I reached a certain town near Gabon and Nigeria. I had a vehicle and I crossed to Nigeria. I just paid normally [not bribing], as I had no luggage it looked like I was just walking, an ordinary man.

"Once there, I tried to link to my family back in Cameroon. I found somebody who was moving from Nigeria to Cameroon, so I gave them a note. They [my family] thought I was still in prison. Because when you are detained, your family does not communicate with you and don't know what happens; they don't know if you are coming back or you are dead. Some try to visit, and if they don't see you in the cell, that's when they know if you are dead or not. They did not know where I was; they were surprised. It had been nine months. They didn't believe the note; they thought somebody must have faked it until they saw my signature.

"Then I tried a phone. They were too happy, and I told them that they should calm down. They ask me how I managed to go on living. I don't know exactly how I managed. After calling, I found my way back to Cameroon, because I could not move anywhere without a passport. I had to bribe my way around in Cameroon. I had some small money in my accounts but there was no way my wife could get the money out. I had to bribe to get my passport and travel documents. It consumed nearly all my wealth.

"I contacted a family friend in America; he was Cameroonian, and told him my plight, that I am now a dead man. As a politician, I had contacts. The friend now built up a letter to invite his friend to come to a political meeting in Minnesota. He wrote the letter, and sent it. I took it, but to go to the embassy was a problem because the embassy is in East Cameroon, where I was detained in Yaoundé. That was the problem: I was between the devil and the sea.

"The day I went to the embassy, I presented my real document when I was interviewed. There is no bribing in the embassy. Let no man deceive you, you are genuine. When I came, there was a small cubicle and the officer interviewing me was behind a screen. There was a microphone so when he talks, you can hear.

"The officer who was interviewing me was a young gentleman, and he asked me my name. I told him my name. He asked me my age. I told him my age. He asked me the purposed of my visit.

"I took a breath, because the purpose for which my friend invited me was not the purpose for which I was going. I told him why: 'I am a retired political civil servant, but my ideas...I really want to go and calm down myself. A friend has invited me so I can go and calm down myself.'

"He looked me in the face and ask me, 'Are you sure you are going to come back?' I paused for a while, because I could not say yes or no. I knew in the heart of my heart that I was not going to come back; my country was not safe for me. I am sure he knew psychology and knew the answer I was going to give...someone who knows psychology knows that when somebody pauses, that answer is going to be a negative answer. So although I said yes, I know very well that he knew the answer was to be a no.

"Then he asked if I was married. He was opening my documents, and I had attached my marriage certificate, but he still asked just to confirm. Then I said, 'I can't go and stay; I can't leave my wife and children behind.' He looked at me—he looked into my face for a while—and then he told me to put my thumb and this forefinger on a fingerprint light. He went and took a form and told me to come back at four o'clock for my visa.

"As simple as that. It was not just him, but God in him—he saw something in me; he didn't even ask me five questions. That was June 2004. There was a crowd of people to come to the US. He did not go with a negative answer; that is why I say God came into him and worked a miracle. If I had stayed in that country for one more week...just as I left the country, they harassed my children, my family. They came to my house, said my wife must produce me. My wife said I had been picked up here so many months ago.

"But they didn't believe her. They went into the house, they scattered everything, they said I was there. My wife said, "Here where?" I don't know whether they would ask the children, but the children would obviously have said, 'Yes, my father has been here.' Luckily, they were frightened and hid themselves, so it was only my wife. They broke the windows, looked in the closet to see whether I was hidden there.

"But I had gone to the embassy by four, got my passport, and everything was there. I saw the visa, saw it stamped, and my friend here had paid my ticket, a two-way so it would look like I was coming back.

"I arrived in St. Paul. I used Northwest Airlines. My friend was waiting. When I arrived in America, I knew that I was safe. I stayed with him and registered with the Center for Victims of Torture. They asked me if I had money, and I said that this is me: I don't have nothing, nothing. They saw the wounds on my back. The doctor examined me. They used knives to pierce you on your thigh, your back, torturing you to make you yield. Those wounds were still fresh. When you are talking, they just bash your mouth all through. They had wounded the gums, cut all the teeth...CVT asked me now, 'Can you write your history?' I said, 'Oh, I can,' and I went through my history.

"They transferred me to the Advocates for Human Rights. Emily Good, a good and brilliant young lawyer—I wish her all the best in her future—she got my history, she just mainly dotted a few i's and some t's. Then she told me to meet her in the office, and we drove to Bloomington. I did not know where it was. I was just moving blinding. She left me now, and as I was sitting there, I saw a young lady, and I greeted her good morning.

"She said good morning, and asked my name. She just involved me in a conversation; I thought she was just an inquisitive person. Little did I know that I was undergoing my interview. She was a twenty-six-year-old girl. She asked me to follow her, and we started conversing again along the way. She asked me so many things, so trickishly. If I had digressed from my response in my written history, that's where I would have victimized myself.

"She asked me, 'Were you tortured? How long? How long were you detained? Were you beaten?' I said 'Oh! The rate at which I was beat was beyond human bearing.' She asked, 'How were you fed?' I said, 'Sometimes my wife brought food; they refused her food and the food they gave us was beyond human consumption.'

"She opened the door to an office and said I should come in, so I was following as if maybe they wanted me to come and wait until my time. I saw her go behind a desk, and then I saw the American flag. When you come into an office and you see somebody who sits with the flag of her country behind...that is when I knew; it pricked me that I was talking to my asylee officer. But it did not bother me because I had not involved myself in any negative response. That's when I saw my file in front of her...I took a breath. She opened the file and asked my name, whether I was married. I said I have four children who are minors, but I have many children who are older. In the African context, as a man, I inherited my father's things and all other things. I have children by adoption. In Africa, your sister's children are your children. As long as you are an uncle, your sister's children call you papa and you are their father.

"Suddenly my advocate came and opened the door and said, 'I am sorry. I was called to another room.' Then she sat down, but she was not asked any questions because I had gone through my interview vividly with no alteration. I didn't cheat. The dates were really coherent, the sequence of my events were easy, and the events that affected me were not imagined. They all agreed.

"Then [the asylum officer] told us, 'Bayongson has been granted a tentative asylum.' It was just about seven days [later] when my lawyer phoned me and she said there is a letter granting me asylum in her office. I had the shortest asylee [petition]...there was not any hitch—no hitch. It happened in God's guidance. In total, it did not take me up to one year—that is the fun about it.

"The Center for Victims of Torture was very useful, and so was Minnesota Council of Churches. I told you that I volunteered here?" Bayongson volunteered as an assistant with the immigration services staff at MCC. "With all my knowledge, I wanted to at least be volunteering. I volunteered too with the Minnesota AIDS project, because while back at home, I was an outreacher in the AIDS project. I had a job, so I created time to volunteer; I made time because I was happy with what the Americans had done to me. I want to give back some part of my happiness."

After being granted asylum, Bayongson was able to work and found a job at J.C. Penny. "In America, no matter how educated you are, you must have education in the form of America. That is how I discovered things. I don't know computer, nothing. J.C. Penny took me to be one of their support staff; I was just offloading goods. Then I was moved—I can use the word "promoted"—to pricing. I was now pricing, because my supervisor saw that I was very instrumental and I could really work. [I did this] until, with the small money I had, I did my training as a nursing assistant. Then, with my knowledge from educating the community through the German nonprofit organization [in Cameroon], I found my nursing assistant education easy." Soon Bayongson began working in an assisted-living home.

"When I had my asylee documents, I applied now to bring my family. That was another process; it takes a long time. I was struggling to get the money—tickets were getting dearer and dearer." There is no financial support for asylees to pay for plane tickets to bring over family members; they must pay in full. "The last cheapest ticket for them to come was two thousand six hundred dollars. Can you imagine to bring them? Oh! It was not an easy thing. At the job I was paid minimally, and it became at a time I was sick, and up to now I don't have any insurance. I am a hepatitis patient, and I was admitted to a hospital, I have a bill there, which is more than eleven thousand dollars. I tried and tried until my family came. They arrived here the 26th of March 2008."

Meanwhile, Bayongson's sisters and other children are in Cameroon. He hopes to bring the younger ones over eventually. "By the law of this country, adults can only come to visit, but I have around four who are young enough. If I do not bring them, my children may be able to, if God says I am not to. I talk to them on the phone."

Religion has been a common thread in Bayongson's description of his life. He talks more about this.

"I am a born and professing Christian; I am a Presbyterian. We are a member at Arlington Hill Church and my wife is very instrumental in the church. She teaches songs. The church is so lively—when you see the African community there, that is where she is projecting her image well."

Bayongson firmly believes that his children will not forsake their

Cameroonian heritage. He says, "I know the adage that no matter how many years you put a rock in the sea, it can't become a fish. If you throw a stick in the sea, it is still a stick. I strongly believe that no matter how long my children stay here, they will adapt to American culture but will still identify themselves as Cameroonians. I am still orienting them, educating them—I am teaching them to grow up in their background.

"The taller twin is playing basketball in their school, the other twin is playing soccer. I used to be a good soccer player, too. I always tell them that when you mix yourself with Americans, don't forget who you are, an African Cameroonian. It does not mean that I hate Americans; I am just saying that a fish is a fish and a stone is a stone. All may be in the sea, but you must identify that this is a stone and this is a fish. That is why I say I try to bring them to maintain my culture, the culture which I am trying to foster, and what I am here for—what I want for them when they grow up—is to fight for the emancipation of the West Cameroonians. We want to have our identity. If Eritrea was under Ethiopia for so many years and is now a nation, if East Timor has been granted her independence, I do not see why tomorrow the United Nations shall not grant us our independence. I know that in the heart of my heart, that one day our prayers will be heard."

Conclusion

It seems almost inappropriate to utter a word after witnessing these brave women and men recount their harrowing escapes and transitions to life in Minnesota. These are the kinds of stories that may leave you speechless at first, but will soon move you to ask questions, to learn more, and to advocate for the human rights of the world's most vulnerable people.

Will you look at the world the same way again? The young man caring for your aging parents in the nursing home could be a refugee who first distributed medicine in a refugee camp in Kenya. The homeless shelter where you volunteer may house a woman who escaped with only her life, leaving her children behind in Zimbabwe and is now doing everything she can to survive a brutally complex immigration system. Your daughter's supervisor in the audio-visual department at the University of Minnesota could be a former journalist who was forced to abandon his home and his profession in pursuit of safety.

Each refugee has a story, an entire life that preceded her or his time in Minnesota. The many refugees who now live in Minnesota were once electricians, event planners, farmers, politicians, pastors, journalists, or held other respectable professional positions. Some have families scattered on different continents. Others don't know if their loved ones are alive. Refugees are survivors of unimaginable physical and emotional pain—yet they survived. These survivors have pasts that are like nightmares, but their hopes and dreams for the future propel them forward. Refugees are living testimonies of the strength of the human spirit.

Yet we must resist drawing conclusions or make broad, sweeping claims about refugees in Minnesota. Their stories speak for themselves, as do the following salient quotations from those brave enough to add their refugee stories to Minnesota's history. As you hear these voices again, remember that these quotations are not just words on a page. They come from living, breathing people whose lives have gone on since they first told their stories. And now these stories will live in those who are privileged enough to encounter them. May these stories continue to encourage, inspire, and move those who hear them to offer greater hospitality to members of Minnesota's refugee communities.

"Before, we are the displaced, and displaced people have no legal status. So now we are so glad to be living in America and get the legal status. We can legally live the center of our lives here, so we are very glad."—Josiah

"I will become a citizen of the United States, and grow old in the United States, and die in the United States."—Krishna

"So that's the way we train our kids. We want them to be citizens of the world. And see the beauty displayed throughout the universe by diversity. Open their eyes to see the beauty. Not to see boundaries or limitations."—Abdul (and Dunia)

"We miss our festivals."—Prakash (and Shailesh)

"Life is expensive here. It is good—yeah, many things are good, but some of the things...it is difficult for us. After a while, I hope, we will adapt."—Januka

"I know that in the heart of my heart, that one day our prayers will be heard."—Bayongson

"We decided to be here for the rest of our life. Even though I still have passion, I still want to go home because there are a lot of people who still need to know the Lord."—Moses

"My dream is to learn to be somebody, to stand to my life. To get what I want."—Munira

"But for me, the Statue of Liberty is not just a sign of freedom. It is life for me. It means life. Not death."—Semantics

"I know the life of refugees, you know. That's why I wanna learn and work with refugees, helping refugees."—Sharmake

"Many families have a different history. Yes. But I have opportunity to tell about my story like this, so I tell you. Thank you."
—Lah Paw

"The country that don't need you there, that is not my country. The country that brought me and said, 'This is your life, you can live here and do anything you want in here'—that is my country. Not the country that kicked you out."—Senan

"In an ideal world, I think my family should come here. But the only thing I can do right now is just to start over. Just to start over, and forget about a lot of things."—Malaba

"I appreciate all those people who have helped me to tell my story."—Maka

"I just know that I am a human; I have to know myself, where we come from. Everyone can live together in peace.—Kaw Lah

"That much I can tell you."—Hiruy

Glossary

The Advocates for Human Rights: A Minnesota based nonprofit
organization with the mission to implement international human rights
standards in order to promote civil society and reinforce the rule of law
in the United States and in select global communities.

Affidavit of Relationship (AOR): An application certain refugees or
asylees in the United States may be eligible to file to help family members
who are left behind to be considered for the US Refugee Program.
An AOR application is filed with assistance from the local refugee
resettlement program.

Asylee: A person who comes to the United States and, after an
application, screening, and interview process by the United States
Citizenship and Immigration Services (USCIS), is granted asylum in the
United States based on the individual's unwillingness to return to the
home country due to a well-founded fear of persecution based on race,
religion, nationality, membership in a particular social group, or political
opinion.

Episcopal Migration Ministries (EMM): One of nine national agencies
working in partnership with the US Department of State to resettle

individuals granted refugee status in the United States. MCC Refugee Services is a local affiliate of EMM.

ESL: English as a Second Language.

Center for Victims of Torture (CVT): A Minnesota-based organization that provides mental health care and resources to victims of government-sponsored torture. CVT's services also include research, training, and public policy initiatives in order to develop strategies for abolishing torture worldwide.

Church World Service (CWS): One of nine national agencies working in partnership with the US Department of State to resettle individuals granted refugee status in the United States. MCC Refugee Services is a local affiliate of CWS.

Karen National Union (KNU): The mainstream rebel movement fighting for autonomy from Burma/Myanmar in the form of an independent Karen state.

Internally Displaced Persons (IDPs): People who are forced to flee their home, but do not leave their country's borders.

International Office of Migration (IOM): An inter-governmental organization that works to maintain and promote orderly and humane management of migration. It is contracted by the US Department of State to manage travel of refugees from their country of refuge to the United States.

Minnesota Council of Churches (MCC): A nonprofit organization in Minnesota seeking unity in the Christian church and building common good in the world through ecumenical and interfaith collaboration, advocacy, and service. MCC Refugee Services is a program of the Minnesota Council of Churches.

NGO: Nongovernmental organization.

Refugee: A person who, due to a well-founded fear of being persecuted for reasons of race, religion, nationality, membership of a particular social group, or political opinion, is outside the country of the individual's nationality, and is unable to, or owing to such fear, is unwilling to avail oneself of the protection of that country.

United Nations (UN): An international organization founded in 1945 after the Second World War by fifty-one countries committed to maintaining international peace and security, developing friendly relations among nations, and promoting social progress, better living standards, and human rights.

United Nations High Commission for Refugees (UNHCR): The agency mandated to lead and coordinate international action to protect refugees and resolve refugee problems worldwide.

US Citizen and Immigration Services (USCIS): The branch of US Homeland Security overseeing lawful immigration to the United States.

ZANU PF: Zimbabwe African National Union, Patriotic Front (Robert Mugabe's political party).

Bibliography

Al-Jazeera. "From Minneapolis to Mogadishu." The Rageh Omaar Report, July 15, 2010. Accessed February 28, 2011. http://english.aljazeera.net/programmes/ragehomaarreport/2010/07/201071583644674720.html.

Baylor University, "Ethiopian Refugees." Accessed March 2, 2011. http://bearspace.baylor.edu/Charles_Kemp/www/ethiopian_refugees.htm

Brady, Emily. "A Year of Living Nervously." The New York Times online. Accessed March 2, 2011, http://www.nytimes.com/2008/12/07/nyregion/thecity/07asyl.html?_r=1&pagewanted=all

Center for Applied Linguistics, "Bhutanese Refugees in Nepal." Accessed March 2, 2011, http://www.cal.org/co/pdffiles/backgrounder_bhutanese.pdf.

Center for Applied Linguistics. "Liberians: An Introduction to their History and Culture." Accessed March 2, 2011 http://www.cal.org/co/liberians/liberian_050406_1.pdf

Center for Applied Linguistics, "Refugees from Iraq." Accessed March 2, 2011, http://www.cal.org/co/pdffiles/iraqis.pdf

Center for Applied Linguistics. "Somalis: Their History and Culture." Accessed February 28, 2011. http://www.cal.org/co/somali/shist.html.

Church World Service, "Karen Refugees." Accessed March 2, 2011 http://www.churchworldservice.org/PDFs/refugees/Karenrefugees.pdf

CIA World Factbook. "Bhutan." Accessed March 2, 2011, https://www.cia.gov/library/publications/the-world-factbook/geos/bt.html.

CIA World Factbook. "Burma." Accessed March 2, 2011 https://www.cia.gov/library/publications/the-world-factbook/geos/bm.html

CIA World FactBook, "Cameroon." Accessed March 2, 2011, https://www.cia.gov/library/publications/the-world-factbook/geos/cm.html

CIA World Factbook. "Congo, Democratic Republic of the." Accessed March 2, 2011 https://www.cia.gov/library/publications/the-world-factbook/geos/cg.html

CIA World Factbook. "Iraq." Accessed March 2, 2011 https://www.cia.gov/library/publications/the-world-factbook/geos/iz.html.

CIA World Factbook. "Liberia." Accessed March 2, 2011 https://www.cia.gov/library/publications/the-world-factbook/geos/li.html

CIA World Factbook. "Somalia." Accessed February 28, 2011. https://www.cia.gov/library/publications/the-world-factbook/geos/so.html.

CIA World Factbook. "Zimbabwe." Accessed March 2, 2011 https://www.cia.gov/library/publications/the-world-factbook/geos/zi.html

CNN.com. "Thousands Flee into South Africa a Day." Accessed March 2, 2011 http://www.cnn.com/2007/WORLD/africa/07/30/zimbabwe.refugees.reut/index.html.

Knoll, Michelle. KSTP.com. "Minnesota Home to Nation's Largest Somali Population," article posted December 14, 2010. Accessed February 28, 2011.

Library of Congress website, "Refugees, Drought and Famine." Accessed March 2, 2011. http://countrystudies.us/ethiopia/46.htm

Minnesota Department of Health. "Primary Refugee Arrivals to Minnesota (Notifications Received by MDH), 1979-2009." Accessed February 28, 2011. http://www.health.state.mn.us/divs/idepc/refugee/stats/refcumm.pdf.

Nobelprize.org. "Aung San Suu Kyi Biography." Accessed March 2, 2011 http://nobelprize.org/nobel_prizes/peace/laureates/1991/kyi-bio.html

UNHCR.org, "Cameroon." Accessed on March 2, 2011, http://www.unhcr.org/cgi-bin/texis/vtx/page?page=4a03e1926.

UNHCR.org."Bhutan." Accessed March 2, 2011, http://www.unhcr.org/cgi-bin/texis/vtx/page?page=49e487646.

UNHCR.org. "Ethiopia." Accessed March 2, 2011 http://www.unhcr.org/cgi-bin/texis/vtx/page?page=49e483986.

UNHCR.org. "Iraq." Accessed March 2, 2011, http://www.unhcr.org/cgi-bin/texis/vtx/page?page=49e486426.

UNHCR.org. "Liberia." Accessed March 2, 2011 http://www.unhcr.org/cgi-bin/texis/vtx/page?page=49e484936

UNHCR.org. "Myanmar." Accessed March 2, 2011 http://www.unhcr.org/cgi-bin/texis/vtx/page?page=49e4877d6

UNHCR.org. "Somalia." Accessed February 28, 2011. http://www.unhcr.org/cgi-bin/texis/vtx/page?page=49e483ad6.

UNHCR.org. "Zimbabwe." Accessed March 2, 2011 http://www.unhcr.org/cgi-bin/texis/vtx/page?page=49e485c66.

US Department of State, "Democratic Republic of the Congo." Accessed March 2, 2011, http://www.state.gov/r/pa/ei/bgn/2823.htm.

About MCC Refugee Services

MCC Refugee Services is a program of the Minnesota Council of Churches (MCC), a nonprofit organization in Minneapolis, Minnesota. MCC Refugee Services is a local affiliate of Church World Service and Episcopal Migration Ministries, two agencies contracted by the US Department of State to resettle refugees in the United States. MCC Refugee Services welcome persecuted people from around the world into new lives of freedom, hope, and opportunity in Minnesota.

Its vision is that refugees are abundantly supported as they move from addressing basic needs to achieving their dreams and faith communities are transformed by partnering in this ministry of hospitality.

MCC Refugee Services accomplishes this vision through its four lines of service: case management, employment services, immigration services, and education. They rely on their community partnerships, faith community relationships, and volunteer and donor support to make this possible.

On the website, mnchurches.org/refugeeservices, you can learn how to connect with MCC Refugee Services, read updates and events regarding *This Much I Can Tell You*, view information about refugee resettlement, and take a survey to help evaluate the impact of the book. By taking this survey you will help maintain the funding for this and future projects.

CPSIA information can be obtained at www.ICGtesting.com
Printed in the USA
BVOW07s2248250813

329412BV00002B/55/P